Praise for Cynthia Heimel:

"**Cynthia Heimel was sexy in the city when Sarah Jessica Parker was still dancing to Devo songs in high school.**"
—Kevin Berger, *San Francisco Magazine*

"Cynthia Heimel . . . gets **funnier, meaner and possibly even smarter, every time around.**"
—Sarah Ferrell, *The New York Times Book Review*

"She's **your best friend, Jewish mother, and analyst, with a better sense of humor** than the three combined." —*USA Today*

Praise for *If You Can't Live Without Me,
Why Aren't You Dead Yet?*:

"Perhaps **our funniest war correspondent on the war between the sexes.**"   —Joseph Coates, *Chicago Tribune*

"**Hilarious.**"   —*Cosmopolitan*

"Psalms for . . . all frustrated smart people."
—Sheila Anne Feeney, *New York Daily News*

"Cynthia Heimel is profound without being pompous, satiric without being juvenile, and trendy without being shallow. She somehow manages to be simultaneously silly and wise, biting and kind. . . . In short, she's the perfect girlfriend. . . . Heimel is humorist **Fran Lebowitz without the snottiness, playwright Wendy Wasserstein with self-awareness, Gloria Steinem with a sense of humor.**"   —Juliet Wittman, *Boulder Camera*

"Cynthia Heimel tears into the fabric of everyday mythologies with a **monstrous comic vengeance.** . . . If *If You Can't Live Without Me, Why* ＿＿＿＿＿＿ **great wit and great truth** then I ＿＿＿＿＿＿ ᴏre."
                                                                tsburgh Press

IF
YOU
CAN'T
LIVE
WITHOUT ME, WHY AREN'T
YOU
DEAD
YET?

IF YOU CAN'T LIVE WITHOUT ME,

GROVE PRESS
New York

CYNTHIA HEIMEL

WHY AREN'T YOU DEAD YET?

To Stephen and Steven,
Teri and Terry

Thanks again to John Crowley for providing me with such a goofy title. I plan to marry him, then leave him. Thanks to Arthur Kretchmer, Arlene Bouras, and especially Joyce Wiegand at *Playboy* magazine, with whom I've had a long and fruity relationship. Thanks to all those people at *The Village Voice* who glare at me from the deep recesses of their cubbyholes, and to Sarah Jewler and Amy Virshup. Thanks to Morgan Entrekin and Anton Mueller, who are better editors blind roaring drunk than, well, never mind.

Thanks to Lawrence O'Donnell, my senior advisor, Paula Holt, quite a babe, and to Matt Wickline, a laff riot. Unswerving loyalty and devotion to Kathryn Harrold, Nancy Lemann, Gina De Blanc, and Sonny Carl Davis. Thanks to all my friends, and to all Heimels and affiliates. Thanks to my son Brodie's friends: Max, Dmitri, Dave, etc. Thanks to my son's girlfriend, Cara. My son himself is just too perfect.

MEN

WOMEN AND MEN

THE WRITER'S LIFE

INTRODUCTION

This is just a book of humor, okay?

It's not a book about an ex-hippie, ex-maniac who is baffled by how strange and goofy the world is seeming these days. It's not about feeling helpless and stupid as these sweeping world events sweep right over our heads and all we get to do is watch endless *Brady Bunch* reruns.

Why would it be? Everything's great, right?

It's also definitely not a book about a midlife crisis, about wondering what it's all about, really, or about trying to come to terms with half a person's sex symbols being younger than she is. It's not a book about a Baby Boomer with a relentlessly slowing metabolism, failing vision, but ever more adventuresome fantasies.

But more than anything, this is not a book about feminism. God, no. Not for a second. It might be true that I remember a time when feminism meant that a woman, although she liked and lusted after men, wanted to be in charge of her own life and her own job and her own carburetor. I even vaguely remember when women called each other "sisters" and felt this odd sort of, well, *kinship*.

And it's also true that I became confused when "feminist" rather suddenly was changed to mean: *A ballbuster who hates all men and wants to see them dead.* I think this happened around the time of Andrea Dworkin–type feminists, that addled and obscure sect which believes that any truck with dudes is capitulation to the enemy and any penetration means rape, and Jesus are they nuts. Total loonies, but the media embraced them, wrote and talked about them incessantly, and before we knew it regular women were backing away, covering their faces with their hands and saying "Oh no, certainly not, I'm not a feminist, get outa here!"

So don't think for a second I'm trying to wheedle and cajole men into thinking of women as peers and pals, or asking women to come back baby, feminism never forgets.

This isn't a book about any of that stuff.

THE
TIMES

SEEN IT,
DONE IT

rent this movie the other day. It's about this dark, brooding, Jewishish guy who's obsessed with death and his romance with a blond, goofy gentile girl who stutters and blushes and repeats herself. I sit through it patiently until the moment where he runs madly through scenic Manhattan because he's realized she's the love of his life and he's afraid he's going to lose her. Then I lose it.

"Wait a minute!" I roar, "I've seen this movie before!"

"Why don't they just call it *When Harry and Sally Meet Annie Hall in Manhattan?*" wonders my teenager.

"That Rob Reiner has some nerve. Couldn't he plunder his own neuroses for a plot line?"

"Derivative is his middle name," says my snotty kid. "Before there was *Spinal Tap* the guys from the Young Ones did the *Bad News Tour.* Same premise."

3

"Maybe Rob Reiner himself is simply a derivation of his father. Carl Reiner is a genius comedian."

"Nah. Being derivative is a trend, Mom. Go with it."

I'm watching TV the other night. There's a sitcom with Candice Bergen working at a TV station full of loony characters. She's playing it vulnerable and endearing and always slightly at sea.

"I am strongly reminded of *The Mary Tyler Moore Show*," I tell my dog, who nods.

The next night I'm still watching TV. There's a sitcom with Jamie Lee Curtis working at a magazine full of loony characters. She's playing it vulnerable and endearing and always slightly at sea. I just whimper.

It occurs to me in a blinding flash of insight that *all* movies and TV shows are derivations of the shows that preceded them, they are almost the same but watered-down, not as good.

Then I remember I had the same exact thought, only better, three years ago.

I'm noticing clothes. We've used up the '30s, the '40's, the '50's, the '60's and we're now enmeshed in the abysmal '70s. I know for a fact that next year, in 1991, we will all be wearing the 1986 version of 1968. Kind of a nostalgia thing.

The newest word in home decor is *eclecticism*. I remember that.

That new nightclub that opened up in downtown Manhattan where the best nightclub in the world, Area, used to be? Kind of like Area, kind of like Nell's, not quite as good as either.

I decide to stay home for the rest of my life.

I wander into a room and find several teenaged boys. They have shoulder-length hair. They are burning incense. They are listening to Crosby, Stills and Nash. Their tee-shirts are Smiley

Faces. They are discussing leftist politics. All perfectly normal. I turn to leave when my eye is snagged by something utterly terrifying.

"Wait a minute, are you boys wearing"—sepulchral whisper—"bell-bottoms?"

"Yeah Mom, aren't they fresh?"

I totter into my room and immerse myself in music. I decide to make a tape of my favorite songs for my Walkman so I can have a soundtrack of my life. I spend four hours working on it. When I listen to it I realize that I made the identical tape six years ago, except this time I forgot "Okie from Muskogee."

I get a brilliant brainstorm for a new hairdo, then leaf through my high school yearbook. There it is.

My dog reminds me a lot of the last dog I had, only she's smaller.

I decide I need a romance to give my life a jolt. Before I know it a wild man is tearing through my apartment and screaming.

"You don't understand anything!" he bellows.

"Yes I do! I understand that you decided to riddle my house with incriminating letters from old girlfriends so you can drive me crazy! Get out!"

"That letter is four years old! It just happened to fall out of my knapsack!"

"Oh, shut up, Mr. Passive-Aggressive."

"No, you shut up. I don't need this abuse."

Suddenly I feel puzzled. "Wait a minute, haven't we had this fight before?"

"It does seem familiar, but I don't see how we could have, we've only been together for ten minutes."

"You know honey, I think I had this same fight in 1985 with Tim."

"Wait a minute, I had it in 1978 with Helen."

I told my shrink about the fight.

"You already told me," he said.

"No, this is a new one."

"I know. You showed a lot more insight when you told me last week."

"What's wrong with me, Doc?"

"Post-'80s sequel compulsion. You feel if you do something once, you might as well keep doing the same thing forever. Keeps life safe in this malevolent and demented world."

"Thank you very much."

"Don't mention it."

Wait. Just a minute. I feel strange. Dizzy. Suddenly I've come over all déjà vu. Have I written this column before? Have you already read it?

NOTES ON BLACK

This has been my wardrobe for say ten years: black shirts, black jeans, black dresses, black trousers, black bras, black panties, black stockings, black jewelry, black coat, black shoes, gray gloves. I don't know why the gray gloves.

Now the honeymoon is over.

Contrary to popular opinion, clothes are not for warmth, not for modesty. If we didn't have clothes, we'd have to wear signboards saying, say, "Hello, I'm a radical lesbian mother with a Stalinist streak," or "Hello, I prefer you to think I'm athletic." But clothes take care of this: Each item screams to the world our innermost dreams and fears. Thus when we notice a girl with a Peter Pan collar on the bus, we can sadly shake our heads at the thought of father fixations.

7

Wearing constant black used to mean:

"Hello, I get a nosebleed above Twenty-third Street, and I will never tell you to 'have a nice day.' I believe nothing on television. Sure, I'll talk about Zydeco music. I cried when Dali died. Don't try to tell me about Julian Schnabel. Barbara Walters is foul. Roseanne Barr, who cares? I was a dweeb in high school. I write, or maybe I paint. I have criminally low self-esteem, body flaws that I think hideous, and never go to bed until dawn. Leave me alone."

Black, the most magical of colors! Black is cynicism and beyond. Black is for people who inanely believe there is a counterculture. Black is the grandchild of beatnik. Black loves truth and beauty, but hates the American Way.

Used to be, if you went to a party wearing all black and saw someone else, a total stranger, wearing all black, you could go up to him and say, "Let's get outa here."

You'd go to the Pyramid to hear some weird band and find out on the way that your boyfriend before last was his best friend in high school and that you were both at that party at Max's where Patti Smith ran amok.

Now the riffraff are wearing it.

My friend Jake goes to parties. "Who was there?" I keep asking him. "Oh, you know," he answers, "a bunch of people wearing black."

The girl at the Alaia shop on Mercer Street was complaining the other day about black-wearers in Texas. "They go to nightclubs wearing black, but it's the wrong black, it's like black Laura Ashley or something. It looks really stupid."

I went to a New Year's Eve party where every single person, no exceptions, was in solid black. Except the hostess—she was in a dreamy pale green Angel Estrada.

Lawyers now wear black. Wall Streeters wear black. People

who think, "The hell with the dolphins, I have to worry about my accessories career" wear black. People who send their children to prep schools wear black. People who desperately want to know the Kennedys wear black. People who liked *Cats* wear black. Everyone at every *Spy* magazine party wears black. People who know what "leveraged buy-out" means wear black.

Wearing black has lost its intrinsic meaning.

The obvious, most practical remedy would be to establish a city agency, a board of directors who would issue permits. We'd all have to bring in portfolios, manuscripts, or tapes to establish artistic credentials, letters from our shrinks to prove we are utterly and irredeemably bonkers, punch in at some time clock at four A.M. to prove we're still awake. We would have to fail tests in money management. Every Kennedy in the world would have to swear we'd never tried to corner him at a cocktail party. We would have to provide photographs of us either a) Passed out in a pool of vomit at The World, b) Marching on Washington, or c) Flirting with a salesperson at Patricia Field.

Then, if an interloper were caught by the Fashion Police wearing black without a permit, she would be fined one black article of clothing for the first offense, her entire wardrobe would be seized for the second offense, and she would be forced to actually purchase and wear only Adolfo clothes for a year as the third offense.

Elitist? I don't think so. More like truth in advertising.

But we can't expect our city government to take the enlightened view. We will have to form our own vigilante groups and prowl the streets. The minute we find a perpetrator wearing black without the proper and correct attitude, we must surround him and point and laugh. This will work.

But even more important, we ourselves must stop wearing black. I do not have to tell you the obvious substitute colors—

you already know in your hearts. For some demented reason, the artistic, the decadent, and the severely deranged are considered fashionable in Manhattan and therefore the country. They will copy us, they will stop wearing black.

Then we start again.

THE CELEBRITY
DECADE?

Earthquakes. AIDS. The homeless. Amazon rain forests.
Holes in the ozone. The greenhouse effect. Iraq. Bush,
Quayle. Crack. Dispossessed farmers. What they're doing
to chickens these days. Oil spills. Baby seals. Black rhinos.
You're having an anxiety attack now, right? I know I am.
Mention even one of the above subjects to me and my mind
scrambles madly for a replacement topic. Quick, lemme turn on
Entertainment Tonight! Hurry, tell me everything about Rose-
anne's new husband's chicken recipe! I must know, right now!

If we didn't have Cher's nosejob to think about, we would
all go stark staring mad. No, really. The media know exactly
what they're doing, focusing our attention on Arsenio's hairdo.
We need to keep our brains brimming with rubbish. If we
didn't, we might *think about things*.

If we had lives even vaguely free from marauding horrors, if we had any sort of lives at all, if any of us even had a meager chance of personal fulfillment or (ha ha) happiness, if we even had a small notion that we had control over our own destinies, we wouldn't give a shit whether Cybill Shepherd lived or died. But we don't, so we do.

During this vile and grimy decade we have by necessity come to believe that unless you are a celebrity, you don't exist at all. If you are not a celebrity, you are inert filler. If the media aren't flashbulbing your every gesture, it didn't happen. Private epiphanies, soul-wrenching despairs, so what, who cares? You are a tree falling alone in the forest.

And so there developed a frenzied desire in all psyches to achieve celebritude and therefore existence. The media, ever-obliging, obliged. Slots opened up all over television; new magazines were created simply to make room for the surging tides of wannabees.

But some of us have still not managed to become celebrities. We don't have the knack, we're always picking our noses just as the camera clicks. Instead we try to be *close* to celebrities, to brush against them, hoping to get some pixie dust on our coats.

Plus, we need something to talk about when we go to parties with strangers. What the hell are we supposed to say to that guy with the ponytail standing under the mistletoe? "Hi, what do you do for a living"? "What's your major"? "Hello, fishface"? No. What we can talk about easily and happily to perfect strangers is how much we hate and despise La Toya Jackson and everything she stands for. And then when we get tired of this we can talk about what a git Terence Trent D'Arby is. Kim Basinger's outfits. Barbara Hershey's lips. Celebrities are our common frame of reference, celebrity-loathing and revilement crosses all cultural boundaries. Celebrities are not our community elders, they are our community.

And I pity them. No, I do. The minute a person becomes a celebrity is the same minute he/she becomes a monster. Sylvester Stallone, Bruce Willis, and Barbra Streisand were once perfectly pleasant human beings with whom you might lunch on a slow Tuesday afternoon.

But now they have become supreme beings, and their wrath is awful. It's not what they had in mind. When God wants to play a really rotten practical joke on you he grants you your deepest wish and then giggles when you suddenly realize you want to kill yourself.

Sly, Bruce, and Barbra, fervently, more than any of us, wanted fame. They worked, they pushed, they stepped on the other guy's face in their desperate need.

"If I can be famous, people will adore me and my nose," Barbra thought.

"If I can be famous, I can get my chin reduced and life will be a breeze," Sly reasoned.

"If I can be famous, I can have a baby with Demi Moore and all my dreams will come true," Bruce decided.

The night each of them became famous they wanted to shriek with relief. Finally! Now they were adored! Invincible! Magic!

The morning after the night each of them became famous, they wanted to take an overdose of barbiturates.

All their fantasies had been realized, yet the reality was still the same. If they were miserable before, they were twice as miserable now, because that giant thing they were striving for, that fame thing that was going to make everything okay, that was going to make their lives bearable, that was going to provide them with personal fulfillment and (ha ha) happiness, had happened.

And nothing changed. They were still them. The disillusionment turned them howling and insufferable.

WE ARE
THE FUCKING
WORLD

U sed to be you could get to Cowburg, Pa. (not its real name, population 2,780) in under seven hours. The train used to stop there; the abandoned station still glares balefully at East Second Street. Then the train stopped running, but there were two buses a day, then one bus a day, then one bus a week, then one bus a month, then no buses ever. But you could fly to Bradford, only an hour away. Now you can't fly to Bradford without going to Pittsburgh first, so if you're coming from the east you fly to Buffalo, then drive for three hours.

This inaccessibility, however, has not stopped the residents from wondering if they can get into Nell's.

"So what's the scene at Nell's nowadays?" asked Ed Bird,

proprietor of Western Auto. "Is it still happening, or are they lettin' in those bridge and tunnelers?"

Ed is in his fifties, father of five, grandfather of two. He was wearing a greasy tee-shirt over his beer belly, a gimme cap, and Penney's Sta-Prest pants. He's never been as far as Ohio.

"Excuse me?" I asked, "there's a place called Nell's around here?"

"No, you know, *Nell's*. On West Fourteenth Street in Manhattan. That Australian girl had the bad car accident with her mother. I sure do like her, she's so sassy."

"You know Nell?" I gasped.

"Sure. I got cable," he replied. "But who's going there?"

I assured him that Nell's, while certainly not in the first blush of youth, was where people went when they wanted a sofa or some french fries.

"Sure," he said, "when you don't want your eardrums blown out at Mars. Well, I got to go home and feed my pigs. See ya."

"Phoo, who cares about Nell's?" said my mother, out in the yard tending tomato plants.

"Well, I thought it was pretty strange," I said.

"I'm much more interested in Brian McNally's new place," she added. She is a small, slender woman with gray hair up in a bun wearing a tattered cotton shirt and trousers. "How's the food? Does Paloma go there? What are they wearing? Is it Brazilian or isn't it? Thank the Lord he's opened a new place. Odeon was so tired."

"I have to go lie down now," I said. "Read the paper. Find some yard sales."

"We have *The New York Times,* the *L.A. Times,* and the Buffalo *Evening News.* Don't forget, we've got to make a stew for the covered-dish supper at the church tonight."

I sat on the porch with the Buffalo paper, which barely had news, it was so lousy with columns. All the columnists started out in approximately the same way: "Maybe I'm an old fuddy-duddy, but. . . ." "Okay, so I don't live in the big city, but. . . ." "Some of you may think I'm old fashioned, not a hipster, but. . . ." The columnists were all ashamed! They felt out of it!

The funniest column of all was by Mike Royko, who I hear appears in New York. He was decrying this new trend in designer labels on the crotch of jeans.

"That guy," said my sister, "where's he been? Those Girbaud jeans are old! Been around ten years at least."

"You get them here?"

"If I wanted to I could get them at the mall. But I prefer Gigli."

"Get outa here! You've never been out of Levis."

"Ah, but I can dream."

"But why dream of Gigli?"

"Because he's the greatest new designer. Up here we're all a little fed up with Gaultier."

At the church supper all the women, who two years ago appeared happily in pastel-hued slacks or gingham dresses, were in knockoffs of knockoffs of knockoffs of Donna Karan. One of the covered dishes was ravioli filled with poached egg, sprinkled with fresh parmesan, on a bed of arugula. I strolled moodily down to the basement, which used to house the church thrift shop, where I once found a pair of green- and cream-striped Christian Dior pajamas from the '50s. But the shop had been picked clean five years ago. Now there was a lonely rack of abandoned polyester. I heard a small cough. The Reverend, a young man in a tanktop, had followed me down.

"I have a great idea for a sitcom," he said. "Perfect for Spelling. Isn't pitch season coming up in L.A.?"

"Spelling doesn't do sitcoms," I snapped.

"Yes, he does," he said. "You're sure out of it."

"What's going on here?" I asked him. "This is a town with one traffic light and the only movie theater within a hundred miles, which is only open on weekends. People used to gossip about the doctor's wife and who threw up on the bar at the Dew Drop! People went hunting and fishing and snowmobiling! They farmed or worked at the tannery. It was interesting here, it was different from other places! It had its own style, its own life!"

"Oh, I see," said the Reverend, "you're into a nostalgia trip."

TEFLON:
A LIFESTYLE[1]

Henry[2] grew up in Clenchjaw, Maryland. His father, furiously Anglophilic, drank gallons of dry sherry and pretended he rode to hounds and shot pheasants by the brace. His mother, stringy-necked from the tensions of being a pillar of the garden club, wanted Henry to go to Princeton with all her heart. "I'm going to art school, Mother," said Henry.

"Don't be a dirty boy," Mother said.

"You must be some kind of poncy poufter," Father said.

The kids at school called Henry a sissy, a geek.

Cleo[3] grew up on the absolute edge of Suburbia. Her

---

[1]Don't for a second think I'm using this word with a straight face.
[2]Not his real name.
[3]*Ibid.*

father, a salesman, was always out of town. Her mother kept trying to make Cleo look out her front window at the tidy tree-lined street of semidetached houses. But Cleo moonily looked out the back window at the bowling alley and four gas stations. She refused to wear her Villager outfits and instead painted a thick black line on her eyelids and white lipstick on her mouth.

"You'll never be liked if your hair is a rat's nest," Mother said.

"But I am a poet, like e. e. cummings," Cleo said.

The kids at school called her a filthy beatnik cootie.

Fred[4], a dreamy, chubby lad from Iowa, had a mother who weighed three hundred pounds and ran a beauty salon in their remodeled garage. His dad, divorced from mom, was the town cop. Sometimes Fred was allowed to comb out a customer.

"You have a way with a beehive, honey," Mom said.

"Thanks Mom," said Fred.

"Stop feeding that boy, Gladys," said his father, "he'll never make Little League looking like a sausage."

The kids at school called Fred "donut head" and "weenie."

But hold! Look! Who are those three magnificents drinking champagne at the most coveted booth at Indochine? Isn't that Henry, the most lauded and lionized painter in New York? And isn't that Cleo, the most fashionable and famous of fiction writers? And Jesus, isn't that also Fred, who charges $250 a haircut, an intimate of Iman? Yes, yes!! Who could mistake Henry's glossy mane of hair pulled into a ponytail, his shredded jeans, his negligently gorgeous gabardine shirt? And Cleo in Gaultier, hair teased into peaks? And the rake-thin figure of Fred, a veritable strand of a human, encased in Armani?

[4]*Ibid.*

Is Cleo crying? She is. She just broke up with her latest boyfriend of two weeks, she just can't find love, something is dreadfully wrong. She goes to parties, meets men, but they come just so close and then they seem to glide away for no reason.

Henry's fingers are drumming, his neck is corded, because he's coked out of his brains. He needs to be, because when he's straight a little voice in his head chants, "Loser! Sham! *Geek!*" Henry's going out with a model now; she leaves him cold—but then, everybody does.

Fred has just been to the bathroom where he stuck his finger down his throat and puked up sprouts and lemon grass. He needs to lose another twenty pounds. Hey, even beansprouts have calories! His lover, Raymond, has recently been unfaithful, allegedly because Fred is uninterested in sex, but Fred knows it's because he's a hideous blimp, a donut head.

Here's what Manhattan is: a haven for everyone who was unpopular in high school. The Village, the Lower East Side, the Upper West and East sides, are teeming with Freds, Cleos, Henrys.

We were all dorks. That's why we came here: We needed to reinvent ourselves. Every sculptor was the town nerd, every fashion designer a wallflower at the prom.

Our friendships are rocky and strange, our love affairs an average of two hours in duration. The soul of a reinvented human is three layers thick. There is a surface layer of grooviness and fast-living joie de vivre. Just underneath there is a hard shell of psychic Teflon which inexorably seals off the innermost layer—that miserable, addled, pathetic person we were in high school, the person nobody is allowed to know about.

Teflon repels—we all just slide off each other. We cannot connect. To connect would involve revealing the horrible hideousness of the peepee heads we once were. Just try to picture that booth at Indochine talking thusly:

CLEO: The boys in seventh grade used to spit at me and call me skank.

HENRY: My father used to laugh and point at my dick.

FRED: Please, God, just let me be popular. I'll do anything.

Of course this can never happen.

SOCIAL
INTERCOURSE

Is it just me? The crowd I'm hanging out with? I've been shocked, *shocked*, by the turn polite conversation has taken. Have you noticed that people will tell anything?

Sunday night, last week, it's Nora's birthday. I've set out kid things—cake and candles, little candies, pretzels—and then a gallon of Rebel Yell whiskey. (This I've discovered to be the perfect birthday party recipe.) There's only six of us. First we talk about how old everybody is. Then we talk about the weather. Then we talk about how many people we've each slept with.

People are telling! Counting on their fingers!

"Fifteen," says Angela, and we boo and hiss because we don't believe her. "No wait, wait!" she says, "I forgot this *ménage à trois* I had in college. Seventeen."

So then she tells every detail of the *ménage*. Then we're talking about masturbation. When we first tried it.

"I was four," says Cleo. "I remember being at my grand-mother's house, looking at a comic book. A woman was tied to a tree and these natives were running around her with spears. I was touching myself." Then she covers her face with her hands.

"If you don't mind, I'd like to reenact that little fantasy in the near future," says Jake, and then he tells how this girl in a bar in Odessa, Texas, asks to spend the night with him thirty seconds after meeting him and how somehow they end up in the hotel room of a drunken computer salesman and his mar-ried lover.

Then Phil, who won't be outdone, tells how a girl picked him up on the streets of Seattle and took him home, where he discovered all her pubic hair was set in neat, perfect little spit-curls. And then her sister came in.

Then we talk about our erogenous areas. Angela said it's first her mouth, then asshole. Then Pete tells how when he was a kid he put everything he could find in his asshole, especially presents his father bought him. At this we all collapse into helpless and prolonged laughter, tears running down our cheeks. Then we all do the Texas two-step to Dwight Yoakam, then everyone goes home.

I went to bed feeling like I'd just been in a cerebral orgy.

Then I'm at a restaurant and overhear two incredibly at-tractive couples talking about this gigantic two-foot turd that came out of this model they know. They all had a look at it.

Then I'm at another restaurant with a huge group of people, and you know how there used to be unspoken *dramas*? Like in *Annie Hall* where they're talking about photography but the subtitles are telling their real thoughts? No need for subtitles anymore. Two of the people in this group had just started seeing each other. This couple, Sam and Rita, were pelted mercilessly with questions:

"When did you actually start sleeping together? Was it the night of Nora's birthday party? Did you go off and screw?"

"Does your old boyfriend know?"

"Does your old girlfriend know?"

"Do you think you'll get married?"

"Whose house are you going to tonight?"

Then a girl told everyone that she saw a close friend of hers at the pharmacy buying a home pregnancy kit. And how she immediately went home and phoned everyone she knows. First we yelled at her, then everybody speculated about who the father might be.

Then Sam's friend Paul started flirting with Rita. He stroked her biceps. Sam was only vaguely amused.

"Do you think you could stop it?" he wondered.

"Come on," said Paul. "We always flirt, why should we stop? She likes flirting with me. It gives her a kick."

"You're the one who's a major flirt, Paul," Rita said.

Their eyes flashed at each other.

It sure beats discussing real estate or careers.

Then we all went to a party which seethed. Old girlfriends exchanged notes with new girlfriends, while the mutual boyfriends stood tapping their feet in stark terror.

A couple known to be on the rocks was observed closely. Somebody came up to them and said, "I've been trying for half an hour to figure out if you're having a fight. Your body language is so peculiar."

"I hate that guy on the sofa," one friend said to another. "He is so dark and negative. A total jerk."

"I think so, too," called the hated guy's wife from across the room.

People can't fuck around anymore. Sexual promiscuity is lethal, social promiscuity will have to do.

THE NEW
COLDNESS

These kids today. No respect. Think they own the world, know everything. Laugh at their elders. Fuck 'em, I say. Let 'em eat bytes. I'll stick with my own kind, old farts, the Baby Boomers. We're sick and depraved, neurotic and duplicitous, misguided and wrongheaded, but at least we're not iced.

I see your generic twenty-five-year-old, and she's wearing fur or cashmere or in a pinch 100 percent pure merino wool, but on the streets or in overheated rooms she's always coated in a layer of frost. Icicles hang from her brow, snowflakes glitter smugly in her cleavage, her eyes throw out beams of refrigeration that could be patented. She doesn't care, she has no interest, it's all the same to her.

I'm sitting in an Italian restaurant the other day, eavesdropping on a date at the next table. She's blond, in a purple print. "Look George," she's saying, "I'm having dinner with you now, but I've decided we're not going to have sex anymore, if that's okay with you. I've just got a promotion at work and I've met a new man who I really like a lot better than you."

I waited for George to turn the table over and become obscene, the only proper response to such a statement. George ate and nodded! This is frightening!

I'm at a party, and it's a normal party, not some weird subcultural event, and the thirties-group are all flirting and then running away, as is their wont. At this party is a large clump of the early-twenties set, and they stay clumped, don't flirt, and one of them doesn't know what I'm talking about when I say I like her shoes. Scientific studies have shown that if a generation has no passion for shoes, it is dead from the neck down.

What were they talking about? Nothing. Projects and pasta recipes. I swear. I wasn't even tipsy, but I walked up to the girl who didn't know she had nice shoes and asked her if she'd ever wanted to fuck Mick Jagger.

"Not really," she said, "although if I could get him interested in this project I'm doing for HBO, I might give him a blowjob."

Jesus is all I have to say.

I know I'm onto a trend, I'm scooping *New York* magazine, which is assuredly planning a cover story at this very moment. "The New Coldness!" *New York* will trumpet, and the cover photo will feature pretty people eating frozen radicchio mousse while starving children outside claw at the window.

I've never felt this way before. I'm confused, I'm ill-equipped to deal with this. I've always figured that everybody's inner life, once you scrape off the shell of affectation, is a seething turmoil of anger, passion, fear, and weirdness, like an Anne Tyler novel. This is why I love Anne Tyler novels, in which allegedly strange fixations are the commonplace and people love each other beyond even death. Now I find out that it is quite possible that the very core of a human being can contain nothing much.

Someone I know extremely well, who is getting a lot of attention at the moment—agent jockeying for position, television specials proposed—used to have a boyfriend. They were deeply in love, it was crazy, it almost worked. "He was a nightmare, but he used to clasp me to him all night long so that we'd actually wake up in pools of sweat and not care. You can always wash sheets, we figured."

But they broke up last year and he is now hustling her! "Yesterday he called," she said, "said he was pleased for my success, felt we should do business together. 'What about the fact that I caught you going down on a girl in the bathroom at our anniversary dinner?' I asked. 'Let's let bygones be bygones,' he said. 'Let's have lunch.' Lunch. *Bygones!*"

"Did you hang up on him?"

"First I asked him when his heart had shriveled to the size of a pea. I am a glutton for punishment."

What would Lord Byron make of all this?

I have another friend who swears up and down that hordes of people have scratched and sniffed the Carrington and Forever Krystal perfume panels in a recent *People* magazine and thus became hormoneless.

I am only one person and not very outgoing, but I swear I am going to run amok. It is a biological imperative. I am going to walk up to representative youth of today and say, "You know what, before you know it, you're going to be dead, you're going to rot and putrefy and feed worms. And you're not even alive, you moron. Start acting on impulse before it's too late!"

It won't do any good.

I HATE
NEW YORK

Can a city drive you insane?

Today I wake up and hope there's nothing to do, because I don't want to get out of bed. My head hurts, a lot. I didn't sleep last night because my bed is near a window and at 4:30 A.M. I heard several men screaming at each other.

"Fuck you, motherfucker, I'm going to cut you, I'm going to kill you."

"Yeah, you think so, ha ha ha ha motherfucker cocksucker? Give me my money!"

"Give me my drugs! Give me those shoes! Fuck you motherfucker fuck you fuck you."

Then they decided to start smashing car windows. Crash. Crash. Tinkle.

"Fuck you!"

So I dutifully called 911, reflecting that this wasn't as bad as 6:00 A.M. three nights ago, when one man was screaming, "Oh Bobby Bobby, don't die, don't die, oh my God, I love you somebody please please please somebody call an ambulance! Oh Bobby, what have you done oh my God, somebody!"

That time the 911 operator was irritated. "Yes, yes, yes, we already have a report," she snapped. I put down the phone and curled into a fetal position, humiliated at having bothered 911.

My head is pounding. Also there is a jackhammer digging up the sidewalk. Also in the apartment downstairs someone is using a buzzsaw, then a hammer, then a drill. The apartment is vacant and being redone in the vain hope that someone will buy it. Nobody wants to buy apartments anymore. Workmen have been here for weeks, wedging access doors wide open. So far, only one family has been robbed.

I dial Weather. Air quality bad. Very hot. Old people shouldn't leave the house. Thus the headache. I take an antihistamine. I feel trapped like a rat.

The morning paper says that murder in the city has soared to epidemic proportions. We are now to treat murderers as "diseased." Will they have a twelve-step program? "Hello, I'm Roland, and I'm a compulsive serial killer."

The phone. "Listen," says my friend. "This Kuwait thing? Maybe they do have nuclear weapons. I'm afraid we're all going to die. I'm really freaked. Plus with the oil, we'll have a terrible recession!"

"We are in a terrible recession already," I say, "only no one's talking about it."

(All my magazine friends are losing their jobs. I find a gloomy irony in the fact that those intensely market-researched publications, the ones geared toward certain age groups with certain lifestyles and disposable incomes, are like lemmings going over cliffs, whereas strange old raggedy dinosaurs like the *Village Voice* swell and prosper.)

Every day I'm afraid I'm going to die hideously and be mentioned in the *New York Post*. Every day when I leave my house I can't breathe, my palms sweat, a strange keening noise begins in my brain.

Five doors down there is a subway substation with a giant generator. My physicist friend says people who live near these things are three hundred times more likely to get cancer.

My neighborhood is going upscale, shop-wise—so good we are losing our amenities, no more shoemaker, no more butcher. It used to be only on my very corner that it smelled strongly of piss, just at the mouth of the subway station. But the intense ammonia smell is creeping up the street; it's about a third of the way along now. Homeless men are congregating and sleeping with their heads in fast-food containers. Drug dealers (I think) place magazines and old shoes for sale along the curb. The other day a street woman jumped out of a doorway and attacked me. Yesterday there was a big brawny man on Fourteenth and Seventh clad only in a pink chenille bathrobe.

I've been crying in the middle of the night over dogs I have had that are dead now, and over how my dog now will someday be dead. I'm convulsed with fear and grief over the children who have been shot accidentally in drug-related gunplay. I'm haunted by the knowledge that pet shops bludgeon sick or just unwanted dogs to death in back rooms. Children and dogs, innocence embodied, are brutalized daily.

I can't stand going to restaurants anymore, there are people with pomaded hair whose eyes rake everyone else to death. They look smug and cruel and are compulsive serial killers in training.

Now that nobody but college kids goes to nightclubs,

there is a new game in town—send a million invitations out for a screening, overbook it by two-thirds, then sneer at the several hundred people who have organized their evenings around this event, who wait patiently in line for an hour only to be told to fuck off.

Last night I saw something black and furry dash across my floor.

My friend's uncle was slashed for no reason in the subway. Another friend had a chocolate milkshake poured over her and her wallet stolen.

It's 6:29 P.M. I'm still in bed. I'm staying here.

IT'S NOW,
IT'S TRENDY,
IT'S CODEPENDENCY!

Hundreds of people were milling in the lobby of the Ninety-second Street Y in Manhattan. Several women were hysterical. "There are no more tickets! It's sold out!" whined a woman in a major mink to the crowd at large. "I must have a ticket right now!" A blond in a boa was waving money in the air, others were begging at the box office.

All to see *Blue No More: Combatting Love-Addiction,* a panel with Erica Jong, Gloria Steinem, Raoul Felder, Suzanne Somers, and Judy Collins.

After plugging her new book, Erica opened the panel discussion with the question "How do you feel about the term 'codependency'?" And the multitudes of women and the sprinkling of men in the vast auditorium audibly sighed and settled themselves, rapt and ready.

Codependency is a very happening concept. Nobody knows precisely what it means. The term comes from those twelve-step programs: Alcoholics Anonymous, Narcotics Anonymous, Overeaters Anonymous, Gamblers Anonymous, Sexoholics Anonymous. It describes mates or family members of addicts or recovering addicts—the people who put up with and/or love addicted people. If you belong to Al-Anon or ACOA (Adult Children of Alcoholics), which are also twelve-step programs, chances are good that you consider yourself codependent.

You consider yourself addicted to a relationship that is bad for you, that undermines you. You realize that instead of putting yourself and your happiness first, you give over all power to someone else, that what they think and feel is more important than what you think and feel. Your whole being is involved in taking care of someone else, worrying about what they think of you, how they treat you, how you can make them treat you better. Right now everyone in the world seems to think that they are codependent and that they come from dysfunctional families. They call it codependency, I call it the human condition.

"Gloria," asked Erica Jong, "what is the difference between a normal woman and a love-addict?"

"Probably nothing," said Gloria Steinem to huge applause. She then went on to be thankful that what Freud called a healthy female is now seen as a pathology. That women who devote their whole lives to another human being are no longer being perceived as normal. And that the terms "battered woman" or "displaced homemaker" were just called "life" ten years ago.

"Most men need the golden rule," she said. "Most women need to reverse the golden rule—do unto themselves as they would do unto others."

Suzanne Somers talked about being a child of an alcoholic. "What our parents do to us affects who we will be as adults. I grew up trying to make my alcoholic father happy. Later, when I was in a relationship, I used behavior patterns that were about childhood. If there was nothing wrong, I went out and created a crisis. That was normal to me. That felt right. I want it to feel right when it's actually right. Oh, God, I sound like Chrissie."

"You people," said Raoul Felder, a divorce lawyer and the token man, "don't have a monopoly on this. Although I wouldn't call it addiction. Men call it obsession. I don't think you can be addicted to a man in the same way you can be addicted to alcohol. Have you ever seen a single cell become addicted to alcohol? It can happen in five minutes, the cell becomes a shaking mass of protoplasm."

"Exactly the same!" cried all the women.

Suzanne explained sweetly to Raoul that the same pain, the same hollow emptiness that causes people to take drugs or drink is what causes codependents or love-addicts to attach themselves so destructively to other people.

"But it ain't illegal, and they don't put you in jail for it," said Raoul.

"And that's the problem," said Gloria as a joke.

Then in some subtle way all hell broke loose. The women got into a fight with Raoul because he was saying that women, legally, were in worse shape than ever before—they weren't getting alimony, they weren't getting custody, that women should be addressing those issues. Then he was accused of blaming the victim, then the audience started hissing him madly when he made some kind of simplistic yet incomprehensible statement about how if a woman had written $e = mc^2$, well then, she would have been Einstein, and then Judy and Suzanne said So what if they call you ballbusters, sometimes you have to be ballbusters and it's codependent to worry about people calling you ballbusters anyway. And I became really annoyed.

Because this wasn't a discussion about codependency or love-addiction, this was all about feminism.

I think there probably is something to this codependency business, and that certain people suffer from its very real and debilitating problems, and that if you come from a crazy and abusive family, you're not going to have the greatest interpersonal relationships unless you're smart and brave enough to conquer your demons.

But I worry when it becomes a fad, when it becomes about gender, when women *en masse* start referring to themselves as codependent. And when there are best-selling self-help books about codependency and how not to be like that, about how women can have self-esteem and empowerment and not be enablers and validate themselves and all those other jargon words, because it's a trap.

And the trap is that these books are still telling women that there's something wrong with *them*. That they're not good enough. They have to change, they have to act differently, and it's all their own fault. This kind of attitude subverts feminism. It turns a woman back into contemplation of her navel, instead of confronting things actively, politically, trying to change society instead of herself.

And what if people follow the train too far and start thinking that it's pathological and wrong to need each other and nurture each other? Where will we all be then?

Dear Problem Lady:

Would you say there's a definitive answer to the L.A.-versus-New York problem?

I just left L.A., it was eighty-four degrees and, you know, sunny and I come back here and the wind chill makes it minus a hundred and ninety-seven. But then I can breathe here. My sinuses aren't thobbing to the mesmerizing beat of one trillion exhaust pipes belching hideous bile-colored faux-air. And nobody says to you "Come to this very important meeting in the Valley and you'll make much more money than you ever dreamed possible in your wildest dreams" when you're sitting in your friends' house at the beach which means you have to drive an hour and a half and when you mention this hour and a half drive to the person on the phone they sigh impatiently at your childish caviling and they're audibly looking at their watch so you say "Okay I'll come," and you drive through the noxious fumes for it seems weeks and when you get to the meeting in the Valley they all say "Well, it's so nice to meet you and what are your thoughts on a show starring Florence Henderson as a gun-running, cocaine-addled terrorist?" And because who cares and you can't breathe anyway you say "God, that sounds great," and they say "Fabulous, well, we know someone who knows someone who we think has a development deal with Flo, we call her Flo, and as soon as we firm this up we'll get you over here again and soon after you'll make trucks full of money, your grandchildren will be able to become full-time heroin addicts from this money, like your shirt, goodbye."

But a house on the beach is nice if you could get one which you can't unless Flo, now you call her Flo, comes through on the deal, although one day you wander into a room filled with canned fruit and bottled water and when you ask about this room full of peaches and Badoit your friends wave their hands airily and say "Ah, yes, the earthquake room," and that gives you pause. Major, serious, full-time pause.

But then if you're a basketball fan there are the Lakers, who are the most beautiful men and rather graceful. And one of them, the one with the most carefully styled hair, the lovely loping run and the handsomest face of all, is, wait for it, a virgin. Honest to God, A. C. Green. It's about religion. And say you see them when they're playing the Nuggets and you think it will be boring but no, the Lakers are losing all through the first half, the Nuggets are looking great and you think "The Lakers! Big deal!" and then the second half comes and the Lakers, like great big kittens deciding to stop toying with the poor mouse, stop fucking around. Oh my God. But then there's a bunch of pudding-faced teenagers called the Laker Girls who do aerobic exercises during every time-out, and everyone in the audience has his binoculars trained not on Magic but on Michael Ovitz, and the scoreboard tells you they're serving delicious Hormel chili in the lobby, and the ladies' room is clogged with blonds wanting to pick up agents, in from the trenches, fighting for mirror space, saying "Hurry, put some lips on!" And everybody leaves not when the game is over, but when Michael Ovitz does.

And they'll tell you anything in L.A. at any time, as long as you want to hear it. They'll tell you they love you and want your children and you're the most brilliant and beautiful person of anyone ever in the history of the universe. And they smile with the prettiest bonded teeth when they say it.

And there are palm trees, which look so pretty against the sky, especially at sunset.

And at the big movie studios they have commissaries where everyone cranes their neck to see if that really is Tracey Ullman and the menu lists the calorie count of each entree. We don't get that in New York.

And while you're at a big movie studio you could wander by
mistake into the wrong room and find yourself in the middle of a
"pitch" meeting, which is all anybody does at movie studios.
Writers and producers "pitch" TV and movie ideas to men in
suits and women in shoulder pads. They start with one idea, but
if that doesn't work, if the network exec twitches her nose the
wrong way, they make it up as they roll along, little kernels of
vague thoughts turning into big snowballs of concepts. And if you
wander in there's nothing to stop you joining in too. Before you
know it, you may have sold a new vehicle for Mr. T.

But in New York we have streets exploding and innocent
Buddhist girls being stabbed in the neck and cabdrivers refusing
to help her. If we happen into a nightclub by mistake, when we
leave the doorman will be lying in the street surrounded by police.

So which is it?

K.C.

Dear K.C.

*Neither. New York is over. L.A. is over. Think Europe.
Think Brussels. Hurry, buy real estate.*

PROBLEM LADY

Dear Problem Lady:

*I went out to California and they laughed at the way I
drive.*

*Actually burst out laughing. I'm driving along the freeway,
I see a whole lot of brake lights suddenly come on, so I put on my*

brakes, and they laugh. I keep five car-lengths behind, they crack up. I look in the rear-view mirror before changing lanes, they piss themselves.

"We're not laughing at you, we're laughing with you," they say, the lying toads.

Last night I asked my friend to go with me to Torrance. "Only if I drive," she said.

What I want to know is: Where do they get off?

CARLA

Dear Carla:

We New Yorkers, just because we grew up in Ohio and got our driver's licenses when we were sixteen, think we actually can drive. But we can't, because we don't. We don't have cars, for years taxis and subways have been our primary modes of transportation.

Once in a while we'll rent a Plymouth for a weekend and drive to Long Island on the LIE, where every driver is as goofy and pitiful as we are.

Face it, we are complete bozos behind the wheel, and that is the only thing about us that Californians, or anyone, can feel superior about. Let them have their little snigger. Then look at their shoes.

PROBLEM LADY

Dear Problem Lady:

Why can't I have all clothes?

MIM

Dear Mim:

The rest of us would look pretty silly running around naked.

PROBLEM LADY

WOMEN

GIRLFRIENDS:
A BIOLOGICAL
IMPERATIVE

Did you ever see a play by a woman? Didn't you think it was
on some strange kind of, I don't know . . . level? It wasn't! Not
to them! That's straight to them!

        Roy Blount, Jr., *What Men Don't Tell Women*

All that you suspect about women's friendships is true.
We talk about dick size.

    We talk about the size of dicks we used to know,
the ones that got away, and the ones that will never
be ours. It's our favorite subject.

Occasionally other topics surface. We talk penile dimen-
sions, then we talk about death and hair. Last night I knew a
new friend and I were getting close when she gave a detailed
account of an ex-boyfriend's oral-sex methods ("Some of them
just get down there and sort of chomp away; not him"). We
then went on to where to get a lamp fixed, the problems of
peeing in the middle of the night, and the difficulty with vene-
tian blinds. Basic stuff.

Are men so different? Some say yes, some say no.

"Women have best friends, men don't particularly," said George.

"I have a best friend," countered Nick, "Robin. He lives in England."

"A best friend in England doesn't even begin to count, lamebrain," I said. It was Sunday, the three of us were parading down Seventh Avenue South, looking for love or coffee. "Best friends have to be phoned every day. Twice a day. When a best friend answers the phone, you never say hello. You just say, 'Well, I think becoming a redhead might help,' or 'That sonuvabitch showed up an hour late,' or 'I'm going to kill myself, right this minute.'"

"Not true," said Nick. "I love Robin like a brother. We talk twice a year. Here's the difference between men's and women's friendships: 99 percent of men are activity-oriented. They do things together. They talk about doing things together. Maybe they're both chess nuts, or cabinetmakers."

"What I like to call Red Sox friendships," said George. "Men can spend hours talking pitching stats, or Civil War theories, or if they're boring, stock market fluctuations. Let's go into this coffee shop, sit near the window and look literary. Maybe some cute broads will walk by."

No cute broads walked by. The boys drank their espresso and talked feelings, relationships, hair, in an effort to prove to me they were sensitive guys.

Guys, I have never met a sensitive guy. I mean really, no-kidding-around sensitive. Guys are just too straightforward. They call a spade a spade, and think it really is a spade. They never seem to grasp the concept of nuance, of detail. Guys are always looking at the big picture. Women make meat and potatoes of minutiae.

Here's a sample conversation between two best friends:

LAURA: His new girlfriend's name is Kelli. With an "i." She dots the "i" with a circle.

BEVERLY: Oh, my God, not a circle! We know what *that* means. Didn't he learn anything from you? How can he be so unevolved?

LAURA: I had a fit. "Muriel!" I screamed, "or even Phyllis I could understand! But a bimbo? Named Kelli? Take me now, Lord!" I saw this note from her, she wrote, "Love ya." Y, a. Kelli with a goddamned "i." He tried to tell me her parents named her that.

BEVERLY: No way. She did it herself. She probably changed it from Caroline. She wears leg-warmers. Blue eyeshadow.

LAURA: Then the sonuvabitch said, "Better a circle over the 'i' than under the eyes." I stopped my harangue to congratulate him on a good line. Then I hit him.

BEVERLY: So, what you're saying here is you're not over him yet.

The above is an important exchange of information. Rife with undercurrent. Riddled with poignancy.

"I don't get it at all," said George. "What's in a name?"

"I once dated a stewardess named Kelly," said Nick.

"Exactly," I said. "Drink your coffee. Stop ogling that girl with the knockers. She wants a man with a Porsche and a condo. She'll eat you for breakfast."

"Women," said George. "You're either inseparable or you hate each other. That woman with the knockers looks very nice."

The woman with the knockers was a monster. A professional girl, a female who hates other females. Normal girls can spot a professional girl at fifty paces. We hate them, we'll never be friends with them, they're the ones who give all girls a bad name. Professional girls want to scratch every other girl's eyes out, in case the other girl was thinking of going near the man with the yacht.

"So what you're saying is: Friendships are more important than relationships," said Nick.

"Friendships usually *last* longer than relationships," I said. "They may not be more primal, but they're more necessary. We girls need a lot of mutual support. *Somebody* has to come over with the Kleenex and bonbons when a lousy bastard with an inflated ego says that he's really sorry, but he needs his space and anyway he's met this dynamite stewardess named Kelly. Friendships are the families of the '90s."

"Except when you have huge fights," said George, "like you did with Brenda."

"I couldn't trust Brenda anymore," I said. "She was turning passive-aggressive on me. I didn't believe her reality."

"Huh?" they said.

"That's a big part of friendship. Reality checks. I'll say 'Am I crazy, or is my boss trying to undermine my position with the comptroller?' And a friend will ask pertinent questions—what was the boss wearing this morning, does the boss have trouble at home or ulcers—she'll get the information, and pass judgment, and I'll be able to trust her. Reality checks are crucial."

"But when it comes to fixing your VCR, you ask me," said George.

That's what men are for!

WOMEN WHO LOVE
THE METS
TOO MUCH

S andy is not some mere and tedious South Street Seaport–frequenting, Ralph Lauren–encased, doorman-tipping dweeb whom you would expect, because her life is so profoundly meaningless, to fall off the deep end of obsession. No, Sandy is a Broadway star with an enviable apartment and a loving boyfriend. She has a life.

And yet, during game four, Sandy lost her marbles. Gary Carter was up. He had on his stricken spaniel face, the one he routinely wears when he routinely fails to nail the runner stealing second. Sandy really wanted Gary to get a hit. Gary looked more than usually hopeless. So Sandy got up, grabbed an imaginary bat, struck a batting stance, and swung along with Gary, hoping to somehow impart her strength, her hope, her eye.

Gary grounded out. Sandy realized she couldn't handle

her addiction alone. She needed a support group. She came to our emergency meeting after game seven. We are:

Kitty, a glamorous girl with a glamorous job, but a girl who has never gotten over the loss of Kevin Mitchell. Kitty has been writing Kevin a cheery, chatty letter every day since he was traded, telling him about her job, her day, her dry-cleaning bill. She knows he must miss his fans.

Molly, who is English, doesn't grasp the concept of the pitching rotation, yet she gets dizzy whenever she sees any Met spit. She becomes demented at the very sight of Mazzilli. The night of the last game, Molly, a girl who wonders what home plate is, had a ticket to *Waiting for Godot,* starring Steve Martin and Robin Williams. She wouldn't go.

Mim, a girl who shivers when Len Dykstra twitches, who worries over the circles under David Cone's eyes, who was the first to find out that Keith is engaged to a model, who believes that Davey Johnson was cute once.

Me, a person who is still trying to comprehend when the infield fly rule is in effect, who thinks the suicide squeeze is silly, and who believes that no man alive has sexier eyes than Dwight Gooden.

We tried to make Sandy feel at home, but we didn't care if she lived or died. We didn't care if anyone lived or died.

"I can't live a whole five months without seeing Darryl's face," Mim said as she sobbed softly into a hankie.

"You can and you must," said Kitty, "you must make your own recovery your first priority."

"This from a woman who wears Met boxer shorts out on dates," said Molly.

"So you're saying I must regard myself as totally important, worthy of my own attention and nurturing, instead of wishing that Wally Backman would shave off that mustache?" Sandy asked.

"Wally has the prettiest eyes," Mim sobbed. "Oh why, Wally? Why?"

"But would he make a good husband?" Kitty wondered.

"I would marry K-Mac if I could," I said. "Dwight wouldn't be faithful. Those pesky other women showing up at airports packing heat."

"K-Mac, the stealth bomber," said Mim. "I know he's wonderful in bed."

"But he's married," said Sandy. "Elster's not married. Magadan's not married. Cone's not married. And, well, Keith."

"Elster's too thin about the bridge of the nose," said Mim, "but he sure can field."

"Ladies, ladies," said Molly, "remember the ten steps. This is the moment when we must develop our spirituality through daily practice. Shall we join hands?"

"How could Hojo have stood there and just looked at that pitch?" asked Kitty.

"Remember the glory days when Hojo used to hit clutch home runs?" I asked.

"Hojo likes Nixon and is unattractive," said Mim, "let's trade him. And Carter is voting for Bush, he grabs his crotch too often, and thanks Jesus for everything. Let's trade him too."

"These meetings don't cost money, do they?" asked Sandy.

"Fucking Darling," I said. "I love him, I want to see him naked, but—"

"Darling has a bigger crotch bulge than any of them," said Mim.

"But fuck him for breaking my heart," I said.

"Poor little Greg, I bet he feels terrible," said Molly.

We sat in silence, pondering our loss.

"Shall we pray?" asked Molly. "We need a source of strength in crisis."

"We could always go on the Mets cruise," I said.

"No good Mets go on the cruise," said Kitty.

"Fuck it, let's pray," weeped Mim.

We joined hands. "Mookie grant us the serenity to accept the things we cannot change . . ."

WHY I HATE
MARILYN

A m I the only person on earth who doesn't love Marilyn Monroe? I know I'm supposed to, because she's dead and was beautiful and tragic. But Marilyn Monroe is the embodiment (sorry) of everything I hate about how men regard women.

In every movie, she played a lamebrain. Men constantly slavered in her presence, but she never noticed because she was too busy playing paddleball and jiggling her breasts, or thinking someone was a woman when he was actually a man with a giant hard-on. She was fresh, she was dewy, and she was completely, utterly unconscious. Here is the message she sent to men: "If you play your cards right you could trick me into fucking you."

And so men tried. They dissembled, they leered, they

smirked sweatily and elbowed one another in the ribs. And Marilyn never noticed, she writhed around, helpless, like a doe caught in the glare of headlights. I hate seeing this.

I hate knowing men act like this. This isn't about sexuality; this is humiliation, belittlement, and can eventually lead to harassment of women.

There is a Texas saying: "The trouble with women is that they have *all* the pussy." And don't we know it. We just don't know what the hell to do about it. If we show we know we have this pussy between our legs, then we are sluts, we are unnatural, we are not *real* women, who must be modest about such things. That was the thing about Marilyn in movies—here was this gorgeous, luscious broad who acted like she didn't know she had a pussy.

We all do this until we know you *real* well, and we may never know you that well. We have, through the years, pretended an obliviousness to our sexuality as protection, since this is where we are tragically vulnerable. Men are bigger and stronger than we are, and if we act like we know about sex and like it, then we're asking for it, for rape.

Whereas men are proud of their dicks, and will talk about them for hours if given the slightest encouragement. Watch a male comedian in a club, and nine times out of ten he will talk lovingly of his dick and probably fondle it, too. Do you remember in the film *48 Hours,* when Eddie Murphy talked about how he'd been in prison so long his dick got hard in a light breeze? Do you remember the movie where Whoopi Goldberg said, "I haven't been laid in so long that when I see a guy I just *slide* across the room"? Of course you don't. It never happened.

Because women are treated as prey. To be treated as prey is to be treated as an animal, dumber and less valuable than the predator.

From the viewpoint of many men, there are two stages in

a woman's life: prey and invisible. After a certain age, when they don't want to fuck you anymore, they don't see you at all.

I am somewhere between the two; it is an interesting perspective.

For years I have had to fend off lines from men like "What are you afraid of?" or "What's the matter with you, are you uptight?" or even the ever-popular "Just relax, will ya?"

This has always infuriated me, because it is insulting to my intelligence to be manipulated in this way, so I'd say things like "No, I'm not afraid of you, I just have no interest in sleeping with you." This gave me the reputation as a ballbuster, a castrating bitch. So then I'd respond to manipulation with more manipulation: "You're a lovely fellow, but I'm in love with Rodney. Do you know him? He's a linebacker for the Bears."

Now that I am getting slightly long in the tooth it's almost worse. Now I have to wait fifteen minutes to pay for the milk in my deli, because there's a young blond with big tits in the store, and the counter guys just don't notice me standing there even though they're looking straight at me. Or I'll go to a party, say "Hello, Tom" to Tom, who is twenty-five, and he'll say a vague hello to the air because even though I might have a pussy, it's not a pussy he wants, and it's as if he actually, physically cannot see me.

This predator-prey mindset has many creepy ramifications. Last night I was at a nightclub, and asked my friend Wendell if he'd seen Clair. "You know her," I said. "She's tall, funny, a jewelry designer." "Oh," he said, "you mean the girl with the big ass and the fat legs?"

Now I know that men are a supremely visual species, and care inordinately about such things as the length of a neck and the width of a hip, but I wasn't asking Wendell if he wanted to fuck Clair. Yet to him, and to many men, Clair is defined only by her quotient of sexual attractiveness. She is the girl with the big ass, not the girl who has some interesting ideas about neoromanticism and who can beat anyone at backgammon. This is belittlement.

Not much further down the line is harassment. If a man can convince himself that we are not whole, separate people with feelings and ideas and yearnings as well as pussies, then he can justify to himself slapping us playfully on the rear as we walk by him in the lunchroom with a plate of stew. And if that plate of stew slides to the floor, and we get down on our knees to clean it up, well, of course he's going to make a coarse remark, and too bad if we blush and feel confused and angry.

My steadfast opinion is that sexual harassment and belittlement are only superficially a product of men's feelings of superiority. Underneath them is fear and who knows, possibly hatred. Men who are afraid and insecure become bullies and brutes. Men who are afraid of or angry with women will bully them and humiliate them sexually, where they are vulnerable. Instead of expressing his anger at a woman directly, a man will make adolescent remarks about her tits, or write a demeaning sexual fantasy about her.

If we respond to this anger, we are castrating cunts. If we don't respond, we are cooperating in our own victimization. What would you have us do?

Okay, I don't really hate Marilyn. I just hate the way she colluded with those who were belittling and objectifying her. In fact, I understand her motives all too well. She wanted love, didn't believe she deserved it, and took what she considered the next-best thing—lust. At least she got attention, but to believe that this attention was a good, positive thing, she had to bludgeon her consciousness with every drug she could find.

So here's who I like: Cher. She's a smartmouth who will appear almost naked on television and just *dare* you to make something of it.

SWINGING THROUGH ENGLAND

Not that this is really what the column is about, but fourteen years ago, when I was a slip of a girl living in England, I fell (thud) in love and had my heart broken for the first time. Oh, it was awful, I was so seriously besotted, sure my feelings were returned, and then it turned out he was one of those guys who make girls fall for them, just to see if they can do it. It was my first exposure to this virulent species of tick, and I never totally recovered. In fact, we keep in touch, John and I. Saw each other last week.

But mainly I went to England to see the girls. Do you know that English girls are the greatest? Not only are they crisp, and witty, and have those rose-petal complexions, and are all completely mad, but they are *definite* about things. No shilly-shallying, no ambivalence, these girls give the most complicated of human situations *names*.

"Well, did he have the boy disease?" Felicity demanded when I related my travails with a certain guy. We were eating spaghetti carbonara in the magnificently cluttered kitchen of Louisa's house in Bayswater, the kind of place where you go through the entrance hall and suddenly think, "Wait a minute, wasn't that a Cézanne I just walked by?" Anyway, the boy disease?

"You know," said Felicity (brunette, stunning), "when everything's just great and you're having a wonderful time and then he suddenly becomes very weird and disappears. It's epidemic nowadays. I believe it was first isolated by Natalia Schiffrin, who noticed that if her friends were looking starry-eyed and walking on air one week, they were bound to be hollow-eyed, pale, and listless the next. Apparently boys are being disappointing in droves these days."

"But why?" I wondered.

"No one knows," Louisa (blond, gorgeous) said. "Perhaps it has something to do with Chernobyl. Now, do we all want chocolate and cream? Or shall we just drink another bottle of wine?"

The next day I called John, my nemesis. "Delightful that you're here," he said. "Unfortunately tonight I'm going to the Hurlingham Club, tomorrow I'm off to Regent's Park, and on Thursday it's the Proms. Lunch, I'm afraid."

"Fuck you!" I cried. "You, the one who broke my heart, can't stop being posh for a minute to see me?" No I didn't, really. "Lunch will be lovely," I said.

"Fuck him," I said to the girls. "I'm not going."

"Go and be horrible to him, which will make him fall madly in love," Felicity said.

"Felicity is such a man," Sue (Ursula Andress lookalike) giggled.

"No, she's not, she's a woman," I said, noticing her breasts.

"She's right. I am a man," said Felicity. "But you don't know Will Wenham's famous theory?" she asked me.

"It's perfectly simple," said Louisa. "All women are either girls, women, or men. And all men are either men, boys, or hairdressers. Stop looking like a dead halibut."

"You've lost me," I said. "Give examples."

"Sigourney Weaver is a man. Jane Fonda is a man. Diane Keaton is a girl," said Louisa. "Jessica Lange is a woman. Mel Gibson is a boy, Clint Eastwood is a man. Cary Grant was a hairdresser."

"How dare you!" I said.

"No, it's perfectly okay. There's nothing wrong with being a hairdresser, and it has nothing to do with sexual orientation," said Felicity. "Very good people are hairdressers. Louisa's father is a hairdresser, and he's a great man."

"My father is not a hairdresser!" said Louisa, shocked. "My father is God."

"Of course he is," said Felicity, "but he's still a hairdresser. He knows about color, and clothes, and cares if his hair's a fright."

"Perhaps he's a creature," said Sue.

Creatures, it seems, defy description completely, and are the best of all.

"He's a hairdresser," said Felicity, "and thank God he is. Most men are boys. Men who are men are probably the best, but almost impossible to find."

"Whereas I, although female, am definitely a man," said Louisa, shifting her gorgeous legs coquettishly, "I even have the boy disease, that's how much a man I am. I get madly interested in someone, pursue him to the ends of the earth, and the moment he shows some sort of interest, I think, 'Hang on, I'm not sure I really like the way you wear your pinstriped shirts all buttoned up, and the way you breathe gets on my nerves.' And I leave them. I can't help it."

"You're a bunch of loonies," I decided.

"We're not, it's an exact science," Sue said. "We've studied it for years. We even know that girls tend to have women for daughters."

"What am I?" I asked.

"You're a woman."

"Well, it's true, my mother was a girl."

"You see, then," said Louisa. "The more you study this, the more your life will fall into place."

It did. I went to lunch. John has just turned forty. His temples are graying. He told me about his love life. "I'm involved with an architect. She was married in May 1989. In June 1989 I kissed her in a garden in Clapham. In January 1990, she left her husband."

"And now, of course, you don't want her anymore."

"Well, it is a bit of a problem." He creased his face into seriousness but couldn't hide the gleam in his eye, and I felt chilled. But then the light dawned. "You're a boy," I thought to myself. "I can see you in the sandbox, red face, poncy little sailor suit and lollipop, only wanting the other children's toys, taking them away, and then losing interest."

In the bus going home, the conductor was tidying his receipts fussily, he was such a hairdresser. So was the waiter at the Indian restaurant who kept realigning the glasses.

The day before I was to leave, a fellow phoned and offered me a trip to St. Moritz, where I would stay and be pampered in the best hotel. He would take care of everything.

"A man," I thought, terrified.

HOLLYWOOD
WOMEN

"There are twenty-five women in this room and fifty facelifts," said Patti. We were at a barbecue in Malibu, on a gigantic deck looking at the ocean. There were a bunch of women there eating nothing. The men were happily tucking into ribs and potato salad, some of them looked good but some had big pot bellies. I don't know what goes on in a man's darkest, deepest soul, but even the fat fellows looked enormously, richly pleased with themselves.

The women looked wary and skinny, with stringy muscles and questionable breasts. Their faces were disturbing. One, the wife of a retired actor, looked from across the room like a high school cheerleader. She was cute with a frothy short skirt and bouncy blond highlighted hair. But up close I noticed an upper lip serrated with wrinkles and skin pulled drum-tight across cheekbones.

There was another woman, a major celebrity, who looked just plain skeletal with her face frozen in a grimace, and a famous comedienne who had an entirely new chin. I kept seeing beautiful young girls out of the corner of my eye, then focusing and realizing they were sometimes fifty, sometimes sixty.

"Oh my God, oh my God," said the movie actress, *"People* magazine says I'm thirty-eight! I'll never get another job! Do you think anyone will read it? Maybe no one will read it! You know what this means, don't you? Tom Cruise won't work with me, Dennis Quaid won't work with me."

"There's always Mel Gibson," said her friend. "I mean, how old is Goldie?"

"I called my agent the other day," said the movie actress, "I said, 'How come nobody's offering me any decent movies?' You know what he said? 'You're too old.' Am I supposed to kill myself now?"

"I guess so," said her friend.

The newspaper columnist put Equal in her cappuccino and stared absently at the long-legged blonds swarming into the Ivy Restaurant in Santa Monica.

"If you look like that," she said, "you're interchangeable. But if you don't look like that you're invisible. My husband married one of them. If you're a Hollywood executive, you have to have a second wife about thirty years younger than you. If you're a minor executive, you marry a bimbo. If you're a major player, you marry a trophy wife.

"If you're a trophy wife you're supposed to be terribly

bright and do something terribly important like run a division or produce, but you must also be able to wear your Armani blouse unbuttoned down to the waist. You have to be gorgeous. Richard Zanuck and Mike Medavoy both have trophy wives.

"The first wife gives you children and helps build your fortune so you can afford a trophy wife. The trophy wife will probably give you one child who is overindulged."

"I watch the Academy Awards, and I really resent them, the new sex girls of the minute," said the movie actress. "This year it's Julia Roberts. These women don't have any sense of their own collusion in the system, they take pride in being the latest wet dream for men. They never look at the rest of us who have been there and been used up. Do I sound bitter?

"I went on a date with a plastic surgeon, and I told him maybe I should do something about my puffy eyes. Well. Before I knew it he was planning on chin implants, cheekbone augmentation, getting rid of the little lump on my nose, then a little liposuction thrown in. I told him people liked this face enough to nominate me for an Academy Award, thank you very much."

"When you watch soap operas," said the Hollywood director, "the majority of women have had nosejobs and facelifts. They all look alike. Some women just take the short route and marry the plastic surgeon, like Victoria Principal.

"But you can't blame women in Hollywood, because there're so few good parts. The three good movie parts for women so far this year were in *Last Exit to Brooklyn, Miami Blues,* and *Pretty Woman.* They were all prostitutes.

*   *   *

"Hollywood movies are supposed to provide us with role models," I said to the TV producer. "How can we possibly feel positive about ourselves when all we see are women terrified of aging?"

"Why would you ever identify with women in Hollywood movies?" asked the producer. "All they ever do is get to play girlfriends, or moms. But look how far we've come. It used to be that the woman would just swoon and then be rescued by a man. Now a woman comes out from performing heart-re-placement surgery, swoons, and is rescued by a man. Women are only allowed to exist until they're twenty-eight. After that they're either killed off or become evil.

"And women are never allowed to have adventures. When I was growing up, the only girl on TV I could identify with was Lassie. She got to run around and do things."

"Somebody told me that the guys who took over Tri-Star threw out all the movies in development that had female leads," I said.

"And that surprises you?" asked the producer.

"There are more female movie executives than ever before but fewer movies about women," said the director. "And listen, famous actors go out of their way to find people you never heard of to star opposite them. They'd rather find a model than someone who has real chops.

"None of the big commodity movies, the franchises, are based on women—like *Rocky* or *Star Trek*. Woman season doesn't start until October, when the sensitive, small-budget movies come out. Women should be allowed to make crummy blockbusters too! Meryl Streep is pissed off she doesn't get paid as much as Jack Nicholson. She would have liked to have played

the Joker. The only woman who could be called a franchise is
Bette Midler."

"I guess because she's never played it for sex appeal," I said.
"Maybe if they never want to fuck you they don't have to kill
you off."

PMS AND OUTFITS

Hello, I'm premenstrual. So I've chained myself to the radiator.

Why? Must you ask?

I've chained myself to the radiator because if I give myself an inch, I'll go shopping. And if I go shopping I will buy something. And that thing I will buy, that thing I find myself madly and irrevocably in love with, the thing that I think I've secretly wanted all my life and only finally had the courage to buy will probably be a brightly voluminous turquoise jumpsuit with epaulets. I'm not crazy about jumpsuits. I've shunned turquoise since I was seven. I hate epaulets.

But today I don't. Today I think of epaulets as the bee's knees. Today I think I might have been hasty in condemning jumpsuits and turquoise. Today I want to be wild and free as the wind. I have PMS. I am insane. Really bonkers. If you live in England and happen to have PMS when you commit a murder, you can be acquitted. England is a very enlightened country.

You wouldn't believe the boots I got once. Putrid green. There was fringe involved, and I believe some silver studs. Maybe not, I can't bear to open the box and look at them.

The buying of unfortunately colored boots is the biggest symptom of PMS. I was having a business lunch with a perfectly awful girl once, the kind of girl who steals boyfriends. She was wearing neon-blue, leather cowboy boots. Snakeskin and suede inserts. Scalloped tops. Tassels. Beige stacked heels. Excruciating. You could kill yourself just looking at them.

"What do you think of my boots?" she asked.

"When did you buy them?" I asked.

"Last week sometime," she said.

"When was your last period?" I asked.

"It just started today," she said. "Why?"

"No reason," I said. "The boots are extremely pleasant."

"You don't think they're a little *busy or something?* I'm having doubts."

"On the contrary, I think your boots are very stylish and delightful," I said, remembering how she tried to give Rita's boyfriend a blowjob at a party once.

Once while in the throes of PMS I had to go to a crucial meeting that would determine my entire future. I had to look great.

I surveyed the contents of my closet and burst into tears.

"I have nothing to wear!" I wailed. "Everything I own is too boring, boring, boring!"

Then I ransacked my drawers until I came upon this utterly charming, tomato-red sweater shoved behind some old bathing suits.

"Why, you cute thing," I said to the sweater. "I wonder why I buried you." Then, looking behind some boxes in a closet, I happened upon a magenta skirt.

"What a chic idea," I decided.

I went through my tights and in a trice found a lovely burgundy-hued pair. A cerise jacket and scarlet shoes completed my ensemble.

"I am a symphony of reds," I sang to myself as I left the house.

Luckily a security guard stopped me on my way to the meeting.

"You're kidding about the outfit, right?" he asked.

"Out of my way, little man," I commanded. "You just don't understand innovations of style."

"I understand that you look just like my wife does right before she gets her period," he said. " 'Joe,' my wife says, 'you ever catch me trying to leave the house like this, lock me in a closet.' "

"You think a bright green dress instead?" I asked him.

"Do yourself a favor, go home and put on a navy suit," he said.

So I did and so here are the PMS rules. Neglect them at your peril:

1. Mark off on your calendar the day you will become insane. When that day arrives, you are officially on PMS-Watch. Call a nonpremenstrual friend to make decisions for you, even what to have for breakfast, because if she doesn't, you'll have Ring Dings and Valium.

2. When you're not premenstrual, assemble a tasteful outfit for meetings-that-could-change-your-life. Make sure this ensemble hangs in the designated PMS area of your closet. Make sure you wear it.

3. One week before your period, give all your credit cards to a close friend. Tell her to lock them up until your third day of menstruation. By then the desire for hideous boots has flown.

4. Keep away from guns, knives, and epaulets.

HAVING
IT ALL

ello, readers.

Sit down. What I say may shock you.

I want to be a man.

Your eyes are bugging, am I right?

"Here's this broad," you're thinking, "who's been going on for years now about how *great* women are, how fab feminism is, how men are just poor, misbegotten schnooks, and now, go figure, she wants to be one of the boys. Dames!"

I have been thinking about my life, and I've been thinking about what my life would be like if I were a man, and I'm not liking what I'm seeing. If I were a man, I'd be in clover.

This is hard to admit but, career-wise, I'm doing fine. I have to turn down work, I'm so busy. I'm occasionally on television, and sometimes people stop me in the street to tell me they like my work. I live in a nice apartment in Manhattan, and usually I can pay my rent. This is all immensely gratifying for a writer.

I'm sitting here, it's 11:00 P.M. on a Saturday night. I'm bloated from premenstrual tension and eating too much chocolate because I'm lonely, I just went out to get the Sunday paper and saw too many couples mooning into each other's eyes. I'm sitting here with inch-long dark roots to my otherwise strawberry-blond hair because not only am I under severe deadline, but my son is a senior in high school, running for class president and applying to fancy colleges and needs constant support. He also needs braces. So I haven't been able to get to the hair guy, or even sue the contractor who started demolishing my kitchen in July and hasn't been back since, which means the table and all the pots are still in the living room.

I saw the movie *Baby Boom* recently, which made me crazy. There's a scene in it where Diane Keaton, successful yuppie, is offered a promotion. Her boss tries to convince her not to take it. He says something like, "I can have it all. I have a wife at home who will take care of the house, of the social arrangements, I can have a family and a home life. You can't have it all."

"I don't want it all," Diane Keaton says.

Even worse was when Keaton meets Sam Shepard. She wakes up after fainting in the snow, and there's Shepard's gorgeous mug staring down at her. At this point I started whimpering into my popcorn. They date, they kiss, they fall in love and I'm writhing in my seat like a deranged person. I can't stand this.

"Why?" my friend Alan, who's sharing my popcorn, asks me.

"Because why does she get Sam Shepard? I want Sam Shepard. Why can't I have him?"

"It's only a movie," Alan says.

I knew that. And don't think I don't realize how pathetic I am, sitting there in a movie theater being convulsed with romantic yearning for a movie star. It's not healthy or even necessarily sane for a mature woman to be living vicariously through the silver screen, like a fourteen-year-old.

The bad time for me is about three A.M., when I've finally read myself into a stupor, put my book down, and turned off the light. Just for a second then I can't escape the knowledge that there's nobody in the other room watching TV or making a sandwich who will soon be coming in to bed.

Nobody wants to date me. Okay, that is melodramatic, but nobody has wanted to date me since last May. I go to parties, nobody asks me for my phone number, nobody asks me for a drink, nobody flirts with me, nobody tries to hold my hand.

This is ridiculous. If I were a man, a man as successful as I am, they'd be lining up. I'd go to cocktail parties and snap my fingers: "You! Take me home and cook me dinner! Then maybe if I'm in the mood we'll have sex!" And they would.

I know this is true because all my male friends say it's true. They have girls coming out the wazoo. If one girl doesn't work out, if she's not pretty enough, or talented enough, or young enough, they just find another one.

Me? Nobody's interested.

I've got a friend who has been promising to fix me up for months now with a media guy. "Get this!" she shouts. "He makes a lot of money! He's really nice! And he's looking for a wife!"

And every time she says those words, my heart sinks. I can't be a wife. I don't know how. I've cooked dinner maybe six times in 1987. I'm mystified about cleaning floors. Buying a new shower curtain throws me into confusion. Even if I could do these things, I don't have time. I'm swamped.

So what man would want me? If I were a man, I wouldn't want me. I'd go for a more placid, domestic type in a pretty, flowered dress. A woman who would warm the pot for tea just the way I like it, who would tell the children to shut up because daddy's working, he's on deadline, we mustn't bother him with the petty problems of financial-aid applications and braces.

Romances begin in passion and confided secrets and delicious intimacy, but if they end well, they end in domesticity, in who's going to take the kid to the doctor and let's have a window box for herbs.

And I love all of that stuff. I love the feeling I get when I'm standing in the kitchen making a man I adore some eggs. And this is embarrassing but going to the supermarket with my lover is my idea of supreme happiness.

But none of this is in my future, because I can't give up my work and turn into another person. Mine is the haphazard domesticity of, well, a man. You know how a family gets all giggly and excited when dad decides to cook, they even buy him a funny apron? I should have one of those.

And I shudder to the depths of my soul at the idea of someone else supporting me. I would be a perfect catch as a man.

Sometimes I get letters from you, readers. Some of these are really mean, along the lines of "Ha, ha! You chicks thought you were so smart, being feminists! Look where it's got you! You've got your independence, but we men don't want you anymore! We're going after the young tootsies who will wash our socks! Yours truly, Mike."

Well Mike, you're right. You don't want me and I don't blame you. But also listen, Mike, fuck you. I regret nothing. I'm miserable because I was one of the first, and I believe that women my age are a sacrifice to the future.

My young monster, my beloved son and his friends, many

of whom grew up with single mothers, have lived without traditional role models since they were born. It's not going to be the same for our daughters. They will have a much better chance at "having it all."

Whatever that means.

TAKE A
CAREER WOMAN,
PLEASE

There's something we've got to talk about. I thought it was all settled years ago, 1975 maybe, when men and women were in the throes of ironing out their differences. Way before we figured out who opened the door for whom, who got to call whom for a date, whose orgasm was most important, I thought we'd already sorted out the money thing.

So I'm on the phone with this guy the other day. This guy is so smart and successful, he is a guy at the top of his profession, and his profession demands utmost perception about human relationships. So you could have knocked me over with a beansprout when he says, "I think when women went into business, men felt a great loss."

"Is this a joke?" I asked. "What's the punchline?"

"No, listen," he said urgently. "I don't think men will ever recover, it was really a blow."

"When you say business, do you mean like executive women, like Wall Street bankers and such, the ones who dress in suits and seem hard and cold and not what you'd consider feminine? Are you decrying a loss of billowing skirts and soft hair and womanliness? You don't want women to appear as shorter men?"

"No," he said. "I mean all kinds of business."

"You mean women just generally working for a living? Like . . . me, even?"

"I shouldn't have brought this up. I don't mean anything."

"I want to know. Tell."

"Well," he said. "I think men want to care for women. Take care of them. It's very important to us. We deeply miss it."

"What do you miss, the subservience? Being in control? I don't get it. What do you miss?"

"I don't know!" he wailed, and I felt my heart break into a million pieces. And listen, I told him. It is my new policy to tell things to men without anger, because anger begets anger, and this guy, well this is a great guy who was telling me the truth I didn't want to hear.

"This breaks my heart," I said, "because the very thing that I need most, that I could never give up, that is most essential to my existence, this is the very thing that hurts you, that causes a deep and unsurmountable rift between us. I need to take care of myself. I need to be financially independent."

"Oh, God, don't listen to me. What do I know?" he asked.

But he knows. I see it all over the place.

I see it in the faces of men when I'm standing at the bus stop at night. If a woman stands at the bus stop at night in

Manhattan, she looks vulnerable and financially needy. I stand there and am amazed to notice the sharp interest men take. They don't leer. Their faces say, "I want to know you. Maybe you're the one for me." It's very weird. If I am instead hailing a cab, they don't even see me, I don't exist.

And I see it in the lives and relationships of friends and acquaintances. Get a job, your husband hates you. Get a good job, your husband leaves you. Get a stupendous job, your husband leaves you for a teenager.

Oh, don't mutter. Maybe not you. Men are all different. Some men positively thrive and grow sleek on their women's successes. But more and more, men's resentment and anger are rearing their ignoble heads. This is not exactly what I had in mind for 1989.

I vaguely understand how men feel. I get a small dose of it when I consider my kid. He's growing up and away from me, becoming independent, as he should. But of course I hate it. I hate losing him. I want the familial bond snug and undisturbed. Whenever I panic over this awful separation, a tiny voice in my brain says, "But babe, you hold the purse strings— he's totally dependent." And my brain breathes a small ugly sigh of relief. He *has* to stick by me.

Is it that men (not you, surely) are afraid of losing us? Afraid that we'll just pick ourselves up and run off when we start getting a regular paycheck? Does it cause intense insecurity? This seems reasonable. We want to bind those we love to us by any means we can, fair or foul. And it can easily happen that a woman with financial independence *will* run off, for any number of good or bad reasons, so I understand such a man's feelings.

Nevertheless, I want to explain my own. It would be easiest if you went to the video store and rented *His Girl Friday*. This movie is a total witfest, pure entertainment, I've seen it at least twenty times. It concerns an ace reporter, Hildy, who wants a "normal" life, so she's quitting her job and marrying Ralph Bellamy. But somehow, just as she is leaving, she is embroiled in *one last story*. She can't help herself, the story, involving murder, is too good to resist. At a crucial moment, just when she must get on the train with her fiancé or forfeit all, Hildy sees the sheriff, who has essential information. She goes after him. He runs away. She runs after him and, with a giant leap, she grabs him around the legs and tackles him.

Now, this is a great comedic moment, the audience piss themselves laughing. Not me, I burst into tears every time.

Do you see? She can't help herself, she has to do a good job! Even deeper than her need for normalcy, for marriage, is this wellspring of commitment to the work she loves. Instinct takes over and she runs like a gazelle.

Or go see *Working Girl*. Many people dislike this movie because Sigourney Weaver plays a career woman/scheming bitch. I don't mind this. At the end Melanie Griffith gets her own office and doesn't have to bring anybody coffee anymore. This of course brings me to tears.

All human beings, even women, have a deep need to perform their work with as much creativity and competence as they can muster. It fulfills us, we feel complete and satisfied. Work can be housekeeping and child-rearing—convenient for all concerned. It can be selling junk bonds. Anything. (Listen, when I write what I consider a good joke, I feel the adrenalin rush from my toes to the top of my head.)

A human being who is deprived of her work, her destiny, becomes despondent. She ends up wearing her pajamas all day.

So when a woman goes to work, try not to take it personally. We do it not to hurt men, or to take something from men. It's not about men at all. We do it because we have to.

I'D LIKE
TO LOSE IT
AT THE MOVIES

want to see a movie where there's this girl playing poker with a couple of people and a dark woman accuses her of cheating. The dark woman, incensed, stands up and pulls a gun. Then the girl's friend comes in and tries to smooth things over, the girl just keeps repeating she wasn't cheating, and finally her friend says, "I can't help you, Sundancette." When the dark woman hears the name Sundancette, she goes all white and weird.

"If I had known who you were, I would never have accused you," she says. "If I draw on you, you will kill me."

"That is true," says Sundancette; and as she leaves, the dark woman calls out:

"Hey, Sundancette, just how good are you?"

Sundancette needs no encouragement to whirl around and shoot the dark woman's gun belt cleanly off her body.

After that, I'd like to see a movie about a bunch of girls who hang out at a diner. One of them decides she's going to get married, but only if her prospective groom can answer fifty incredibly arcane questions about shoe designers. Not only will the groom have to catalogue the entire works of Manolo Blahnik and Robert Clergerie, he will also have to identify the shoes of Maud Frizon and Roger Vivier by fondling them in the dark. All the girls at the diner think this is right and proper.

To cap off a perfect evening, I'd like to see the story of a reprobate genius girl who is crude and lustful and alcoholic but unbelievably gifted, and who is led to her death by a woman who is so envious of and tortured by the girl's talent that she spends her declining years in a psychotic state, eating sweets and calling out the gifted girl's name.

Yes, I know, I know, don't say it. There are plenty of movies now about strong women, women who shoulder monstrous burdens, who take on impossible odds and win. Women who are stalwart, invincible.

The hell with these women, I say. Don't pat me on the head and take me to see Sigourney Weaver in *Aliens*. Sure, she looks great holding a gigantic gun and zapping giant lobsters. And I'd love to have her around if ever I were in deepest space and some *thing* wanted to set up light housekeeping in my stomach. But I wouldn't want to have her over for a martini and a chat. She has no personality.

I guess it was in the '60s, when movies got good for a while, that Hollywood stopped doing heroes. Instead of larger-than-life, impossibly virtuous hunks, antiheroes were created. Donald Sutherland and Elliott Gould cavorting irreverently through *M*A*S*H,* Jack Nicholson, Peter Fonda, and Dennis Hopper getting stoned and outrageous in *Easy Rider,* Dustin Hoffman in the throes of lust for a mother *and* her daughter in *The Graduate.*

So don't gesture proudly at Sigourney. I want to see women who are rowdy and difficult, who are not victims, who control their own destinies, who are prey to lust and confusion and unbelievable fuck-ups, who are complex, who are real, who are adventuresome, whose entire existence does not rely on the way in which their men treat them.

Don't show me Sally Field in *Places in the Heart;* she was a prim jerk. There was John Malkovich, all blind and gorgeous, stumbling through her house in a most vulnerable fashion, and Sally never wanted to fuck him. It would have been so easy that time he came into the room by mistake, when he got embarrassed and flustered, for Sally to get out of the bath and press her naked wet body up against him. I would have. Everybody I know would have. But instead, Sally had to play the widow virgin. Most tedious.

Jessica Lange in *Country*! All righteous indignation and poignant motherhood. Sam Shepard leaves because he is weak and confused and humiliated by his failure at breadwinnerdom. And she just hangs in there, without once fucking up or acting weird. Women are not really like this.

It's okay if the women are loose and complicated as long as something bad happens to them at the end. Frances Farmer goes mad; Karen Silkwood is killed; Cher in *Mask* loses her only love, her only child. Shirley MacLaine in *Terms of Endearment* loses her only love, her only child, and all she is is sharp-tongued. Why can't we ever get away with anything?

There are, of course, exceptions, though I can't think of any at the moment but that sublime movie *Desperately Seeking Susan,* where the women are difficult, have adventures, make things happen. The men in this movie all react to the whims and caprices of these quirky broads. They're tough, they're real, they like to get laid.

But mostly what I see when I go to the movies is Meryl

Streep being victimized. Or Robert Redford deciding between a good woman and a bad woman.

We are not all either passive schoolteachers or Jezebels! It's always the man who has the impossible dream, who rebels against the strictures of society, who fights desperately to be true to himself. The women are the ones who won't take the risk, who hold their men back, who are slaves to convention. Or else they ruin men with their depravity and lust.

Men still control the money in Hollywood.

If I had my own movie studio, here's what I'd do: I would remake all Jack Nicholson movies with a woman in the lead. Jack is the quintessential antihero. Picture *Five Easy Pieces* starring Goldie Hawn as a lapsed concert pianist who is so tortured by the ironies of life that she has to pick up Matt Dillon at a bowling alley and fuck his brains out. *One Flew over the Cuckoo's Nest* with Diane Keaton inciting all the mental patients to run amok. *Prizzi's Honor* with Kathleen Turner giving it to Jack in the neck. *Heartburn* with Meryl Streep sinister and confused and having affairs and Jack abandoned and betrayed.

And I would make $100,000,000 (net), because it is largely women who decide which movie to go to. This is one of the small powers we have over men, since men know that left to their own devices, they would just see *The Wild Bunch* and *The Great Escape* over and over again, so they let us decide. Wait! I know: a remake of *The Magnificent Seven* with Barbra, Goldie, Meryl, Kathleen, Jessica . . .

WE'RE GONNA
GET YOU,
SUCKERS

I thought I'd get my nails done, so I went to one of those nail salons. I figured that since a Nails R Us or a Nails for Days has opened on every street corner of metropolitan U.S.A., there might be something to it. Not that I hold with manicures, I find them pointlessly evanescent. But my neighbor, Mrs. Fishbein, who *does* have beautiful nails and a doting husband, constantly encouraged me to try it. And you fellas like to be a fly on the wall when we gals are getting all pink and cozy and pretty and chatty. And I needed a column.

So I duly walked into Nailward Ho! on my corner. "Hello," I said to the pretty, scantily clad Korean receptionist.

"About fucking time," she snarled. I stood perplexed. Then she shook herself and beamed. "What can I do for you today?"

"Well," I exhaled, "you know those, I think they're called 'French' manicures, where they paint white on the tip of the nail and . . ."

She pointed to a manicure table where sat a gum-chewing blond bombshell whose nails were, I swear, two inches long. "Oh, just sit the cocksuck down," she snapped.

Well. I sat the cocksuck down. "I think I'd like a French manicure," I said to the bombshell.

She leaned forward, exposing cleavage. "Call me Shirl," she said. "Don't you think manicures are pointlessly evanescent?" I gaped, speechless.

"Listen, doll, just follow me, now you're finally here," she said. "I got something with your name on it." She took my hand and went to a corner of the salon, reached over to a bottle of Persian Melon polish and twisted it. The wall fell away; we were in an elevator.

We descended quickly, silently, into the earth. The doors opened. There was deafening noise, smoke. The smoke cleared, revealing a target range. Two dozen women in camouflage fatigues and headphones were aiming automatics at paper replicas of men. *Bang! Bang!* The groin area of every replica was blown away.

"Very nice, girls," I heard a familiar voice say. I turned and almost fell over.

"Mrs. Fishbein! What are you doing here? God, what is all this?"

"Hello, Tottela, so you finally made it to our little hen party. Shirl, get this young lady a chair and some Sara Lee or she's gonna pass out.

"It's simple, honey," she continued as I tottered to a seat. "The men are right. We hate them. We are going to subjugate or kill them and take over the world. And we're ready to give it to those bums. Put your head between your knees."

"Wait, so this isn't a nail salon?"

"What, you're crazy? You think the demand for manicures is such that we need a shop on every corner? You want a manicure, go to a hairdresser. You want to overthrow masculine oppression, come here. Each nail salon is one cell of our vast, all-powerful conspiracy. We are organized. We are deadly."

"Mrs. Fishbein, you're a housewife. You cook flanken every Tuesday night. You're devoted to your husband."

"Harold? That pisher who farts in his sleep? Oh, darling, you know all women are diesel dykes. Aren't we Shirl?" She playfully tweaked the bombshell's nipple.

Shirl giggled and she handed me something. Something black, and hard, and cold. Something with my name on it. "A Beretta P92SB," she said. "Ain't it cute? Holds fifteen rounds, shoots jacketed hollow-points. This week we tell them they're not in touch with their feelings, next week we blow their fucking heads off. More coffee cake?"

A frail Korean teenager carrying a load of schoolbooks came running up.

"Mistress Medusa! Has the How Not to Have an Orgasm workshop started yet?"

"Ten minutes, Kali," said Mrs. Fishbein. She looked at me sheepishly. "They want to call me Mistress Medusa, I don't mind. Who ever heard of a revolutionary named Estelle?"

"How not to have an orgasm?"

"Of course," said Kali, "psychological warfare at its utmost. We close our eyes and think of old jockstraps, thus ensuring no sexual excitement. Then we *pretend* to have orgasm."

"Drives them to suicide," said Shirl. "They know we're faking it, we know we're faking it. But what can they do? Sue? No. They kill themselves."

"No American woman has had an orgasm since February 1953," said Mrs. Fishbein.

"At least not penis-induced," said Kali. "That's such a very pretty blouse. Where did you get it?"

"I don't know," I said. "So what about all the women in the world who talk about how they love men, how they're feminists but *humanistic* feminists, how they want husbands and children? How about all the women who cry when he doesn't call? Who are desperate about the male shortage?"

"Oh, come off it," said Shirl.

"Don't be a dweeb," said Mistress Medusa.

"Clever propaganda while we work our destruction," said Kali. "Ninety-six percent of American womanhood is now organized and ready."

"Why am I the last to know about this?" I wondered.

"Feminists got no grooming, your cuticles are a mess, you never drop by," said Shirl.

The receptionist appeared. "The Asa Baber Study Group has to be canceled for lack of interest again," she said.

"Pity," said M.M., "I suspect that pseudo-sensitive wuss may be the only one who's on to us. Come the revolution, he's the first to go."

"Wait!" I cried, suddenly horrified. "What about Mel Gibson?"

"You can keep him as a pet if you like," said Kali. "Oh, Mistress Medusa, five women have become inchers today."

"Capital," said M.M., "a mitzvah."

"I don't understand," I said.

"Nails, of course," said the receptionist. "The longer your nails, the more are your destructive skills. When you can reduce five men to gibbering morons in under an hour, you earn your inch. Two-inchers can lay waste to an even dozen. Of course, a woman with a rhinestone imbedded in her nail is licensed to kill. You didn't think it was cosmetic?"

"Consider," said Kali. "All these salons are run by Koreans. It was at the Olympics in Seoul where we unveiled our Supreme Sister, with nails like stilettos and the legs of ten gazelles."

Flo-Jo!

And here I thought you men were just being paranoid.

Dear Problem Lady:

I used to have a friend. Well, I still have her, but now she's got a boyfriend.

And a very nice boyfriend too, cute and smart and almost solvent.

We used to be single girls together, my friend and I. We saw each other through the hell of going to hideous parties when all we wanted to do was lie around in our nightgowns, through the humiliation and horror of waiting for the phone to ring, through making hopeless dates with psychopaths and then going hysterical and spending half our annual salaries on outfits for these dates.

We held each other up during crying spells, supported each other through poisonous bouts of low self-esteem. We were pals.

So of course things have changed. And listen, I was prepared. I knew there'd be a certain quantity of "we"-speak to contend with, that there'd be no more phoning at two A.M., no more Saturday night video- and cheesecake-fests.

But I wasn't prepared for her turning into a smug, patronizing motherfucking asshole.

Goddammit! Just last week she said, "Women should stop feeling like they need men. They should be complete within themselves." He had his arm around her at the time. Then on the phone yesterday she told me, "Men can smell desperation, maybe you need to go away for a while and get perspective."

"Suddenly you're the big expert?" I said. "Now that you've found a boyfriend you are a genius?"

"I can understand your pain," she said.

"Fucking right you can understand it," I told her. "Until two months ago you were right there in it with me, Little Missus Snot. Sweet and available guys are an endangered species, and now that you're lucky enough . . ."

"Luck had nothing to do with it," she said. "I was just in the right psychological space . . ."

"Oh, blow me," I said, and slammed down the phone.

I hate her guts. But then again, I miss her.

LUCY

Dear Lucy:

Consider yourself fortunate. You really have no choice but to hate your friend, and luckily enough she's given you logical reason.

We're only human. And being human means being an animal. And being an animal means that when another animal gets something we want, whether it be a big bone or a big boner, we have this enormous need to rip her throat out.

Of course you're jealous! Even Mother Theresa would be jealous! Life's not fair! Life sucks! How come she gets a boyfriend? You're just as pretty as she is! Am I right, or am I right?

But these feelings are not socially acceptable, God knows why. So you channel these feelings to where they seem more appropriate. Her smugness wouldn't bother you nearly so much without the charge of jealousy. If you weren't so furious, you'd just laugh at her and tell her to get over herself and find out if Mr. Boyfriend has any nice friends.

Acknowledge the truth and be free.

PROBLEM LADY

Dear Problem Lady:

Okay, let's get down to it: What about condoms?

I'm a guy with a libido. And I've been celibate for a long time now because I don't want to die. But you've got to live.

Condoms, I hear, are safe when used properly. I know all about only putting them on when fully erect, I know about squeezing the air out of the little nipple at the bottom so they won't explode in the heat of passion. Here's what I don't know—how to explain myself.

What's the etiquette here? I mean, without even opening my mouth, just simply by the fact of reaching for that little membrane of lambskin, I may as well be saying to a girl, "Listen, I don't know where you've been, and for all I know you've got a fatal disease, and yes, I want to fuck you but I don't trust you."

No girl wants to hear this at an intimate moment unless she's awfully strange. I don't know any strange girls. I know dumb girls. I mean I know smart girls too, but somehow I get turned on by the dumb ones. But anyway. How can I defuse this potentially desire-destroying situation? I mean, I can just picture the model I have my eye on now taking one look at me sliding on a condom and throwing a lamp at my head.

LANCE *(a pseudonym)*

Dear Lance:

And an evocative pseudonym at that. We'll get to the condoms at the moment. But first, what's all this about dumb girls?

Lance! Examine your innermost psyche! Give smart girls a chance! We're not so bad! So what if we sometimes spoil your punchlines? Who cares if we don't stare up at you with mute adoration? We can help you out of a jam, we can entertain you when you're sad, and we know exactly why you want to wear condoms, and we agree.

Okay Lance, break my heart if you must. Here's what you say:

"Listen honey, I'm pretty sure, 99 percent sure in fact, that I'm pure and untainted. My doctor says I'm the healthiest specimen he's ever seen, the blood pressure of a two-year-old. But hey, seven years' incubation period is a long time, and I'm not a saint, and you never know. So I'll just wear this, and you won't have to worry, you tall bony pea-brained sex goddess, you."

Just a suggestion.

PROBLEM LADY

MEN

BOYS ON
THE BRINK

"I don't think I have any friends who aren't virgins," said Alan.

"Most, well, a lot of my friends aren't virgins," said Evan.

"You hang out with older guys," said Mark.

"At this age of sexual inexperience, the most attractive aspect of a girl is willingness," continued Alan.

I was naturally agog, but then they broke off talking to contort their hands. Sixteen-year-old boys do a lot of strange things with their hands. Right now they were flapping their hands violently at the wrist so that the fingers made a snapping sound.

"My mom can't do this at all," said my son (who for the purposes of this piece would like to be called Mark) as he and his friends stood in a semicircle flapping and snapping.

"I don't care about that, I want to hear more about girls," I said. Being a mother of a teenager is a strange and precarious exercise, you both know about sex, but nobody's talking. Better to talk about cannibalism.

But I've known Alan and Evan since they were grimy-handed and milky-faced seven-year-olds with watercolor stains on the cuffs of their cotton pullovers. And I've been carefully cultivating them all these years—feeding them chocolate milk and letting them watch TV until dawn—so that when this day finally came I could force them to tell me about their sex lives.

"You can't tell your mother things about sex," said Evan. "A mother has her own problems with PMS and all. Plus, it's your *mother!*"

"I am not opening my mouth," said Mark.

"Girls are people, maybe," said Evan, a baby-faced hulk with bleached hair. "Most boys my age don't think about the true value of a woman. They just think about sex." He stretched his hands wildly above his head in an enormous yawn and knocked over a vase of flowers. "That's how suave I am with the womenfolk," he said.

"There was this girl," said Alan, who is blond and intense. "We told her we were NYU drama students. We thought we could pull it off."

"She was very sexual," said Evan. "She offered me, Alan, and this other kid . . ."

"Let's just say a motel, tequila, and fun and pleasure entered into it," said Alan. "Anyway she was just leading us on. We found out later that she has herpes."

"She was aggressive," said Evan.

Aggressive?

"There's one kind of girl you have sex with," said Alan, "another kind of girl you have a crush on."

Oh, guys, please, don't tell me this.

"The girls I have liked I have only liked from a distance," said Alan. "None of them have been aggressive. Sweet girls. But the girls I go out with are pretty aggressive. I'm a nervous guy. I guess it's not a big deal getting rejected, you forget about it in a month. But I've only asked a girl out about five times. I just can't bring myself to do it. So if a girl sits on my lap and wiggles her . . . ah . . . well, it's easier to ask her out.

"I'll think a long time before I ask a girl out," said Evan.

"I'll do it if I will myself to do it," said Alan.

"I refuse to answer anything," said Mark.

"That's why sluts are easier," said Evan.

Sluts? Oh my God. Still? Readers, I had hopes for this generation. Sons of the women's movement, sons of single mothers, sons of women with demanding careers. Sluts? Has anything changed? What about feminism?

"Throw it out the window," said Alan.

"Well, it's silly that women should be paid less for the same job as a man," said Evan.

"She shouldn't have the job in the first place," said Alan. "Only kidding."

"But I'm not changing diapers," said Evan. "In a theoretical sense I would, but I don't like children."

"Remember in Lucy's class?" Alan asked Mark. "She was reading us *Charlie and the Chocolate Factory* and I stole your comb and you hit me and she threw *me* out of class? Me? Remember that, smegma head?"

"Bogey-bum," said Mark.

"We're not exactly grown-up yet," said Alan.

We went to a restaurant and they made plenty of jokes about the blowfish on the menu.

"Why can't women give gifts to men?" asked Evan. "Why do we always . . ."

"I've never given a gift to a woman," said Alan.

"What about those earrings?" asked Mark.

"What about that bracelet?" asked Evan.

"You know, I stay away more from the women I like than I stay away from the sluts," said Alan. "There was this girl I really liked, and she liked me. I got so freaked out every time I saw her I would go away. I just started acting like an asshole so she wouldn't come near me. Her smile drives me crazy."

"It's a lot harder to talk to a girl you *really* like. It's easy with easier girls," said Evan. "Although I think girls should talk about their sexuality. I'm mature. I live with my mother and know how a woman acts. Girls like it when I tell them I'm a virgin."

Suddenly they were all pressing their palms together and making snaky movements.

All this hand-playing is extremely symbolic, boys.

"Very phallic," said Evan.

"Very Freud," said Mark.

"In junior high sluts got attention, we were just breaking into masturbating then," said Evan.

"They just get hated now," said Mark.

"The girl I'm in love with," said Alan, "if she brought up sex I'd probably say no, because we're not ready. Even in this day and age I think it should be special. Especially the first time. I also think right now we can't think straight."

"We're sixteen years old," said Evan, "and let me tell you, our hormones are more active than our brain cells."

BONNIE
LASSIES

We are in a tiny village in the middle of nowhere, Scotland, and the guys are scoping for babes at the local pub. I am helping.

"There's kind of a Frenchie-looking one," I say to Mike.

"Her hair's too done, she's wearing too much makeup," says Mike.

"Too old," says my son.

At which I sniff. Too old, indeed! They should know from old.

Old is Pat, my new eighty-three-year-old friend who escorted me to the wine-tasting hillbilly hoe-down.

This is a helluva town. Very picturesque, very old, very *Local Hero.* A four-pub, two-butcher, one-green-grocer kind of a village with a good graveyard. There is a barley warehouse down the hill (to start off the Scotch). And because we are in Fife, golf capital of the universe, No Golfing signs have to be posted in every small park. Local girls wear enormously high white heels with blue jeans and feel very glam. Every year this town has a big festival. There are pram races, granny sack races, games, contests, and Scottish music wafting from every pub, every village hall.

I first saw Pat when I peered through her window: a slight, pixie-faced woman in patched jacket and frayed trousers, hair straight and gray and chin-length, eating her dinner, reading a detective novel. I knocked on the window. She turned and rushed to the door and said, "Come in, you're the American in the Weaver's House. Sit down and I'll make you coffee. Will you pick me up at eight o'clock tonight? Wait until you see what I'm wearing." She told me funny stories about Jesus and wore a sly, shy smile. I became her devoted slave.

We walked up the hill to the hoe-down wine-tasting. Pat was a pioneer woman swathed in pink, I was a Dallas cowgirl. The rest of the village, crammed into the hall, were wearing neckerchiefs, straw hats, and gingham. The women wore pigtails. The men had used their wives' eyebrow pencils to draw hillbilly stubble on their cheeks. I drank elderflower and black currant wine, grew dizzy, and found myself onstage wearing someone's straw hat and singing "Oklahoma!"

Beatrice, gray-haired, over sixty, got onstage and did an outrageous version of "I'm Just a Gal Who Can't Say No." She pouted, she shimmied, she batted her eyelashes coyly.

Angie, closer to seventy, allowed herself to be made up as Dolly Parton. Blond wig, big lips, stuffed bazooms, a garter belt, and a furry thing with a tail, God knows what it was, tucked in at the crotch. She became enamored of her new look and threw up her skirt at every opportunity.

"This," I said to Pat, "is brilliant satire! They're parodying sex objects! They're pointing out a basic irony of women's lives: the very same behavior which is perceived as luscious and erotic when you're twenty becomes grotesque and unseemly when you're no longer deemed desirable! How courageous! American women would never be so open!"

"I expect they're just tipsy," Pat answered serenely.

But now I'm at the pub closely scrutinizing a young girl's buttocks. "Now, I think she's really pretty," I say.

"Well, she's okay, but she's not a babe," says Mike. "You gotta have a babe."

"Don't you know *anything* Mom?" says my kid.

"I don't like really big breasts, and I like a tight little butt," says Mike.

"Babe alert, babe alert," intones my son as a delicately pretty redhead oozes into the room. There is a startled-fawn look to her eyes.

"She looks like a startled fawn," I say.

"We like innocence," says Mike.

"God, give me strength," I say. "Is Linda a babe?"

"Not at the moment," says Mike.

Linda lives next door. She is thirty-one. She has a strong, freckled face and close-cropped hair, a solid, compact body. She is either hanging out laundry, cooking, organizing village activities, or taking care of her fourteen-year-old daughter, who has scoliosis. Her garden is suffering, and she's worried about it. Her daughter is about to go into the hospital for another operation.

"If you hear a lot of screeching and carrying on in a few

minutes," Linda told us earlier that day, "don't worry about it. The hospital just gave us a date. She doesn't know it yet. I have to tell her. Oooh, I'm nervous."

Linda's daughter is very tiny, looks maybe ten years old, with a hopeful face. She carries herself with dignity. Last time I saw her she was wearing expertly applied blue eyeshadow. She wants to be a babe.

"Is Emma a babe?" I ask.

Mike considers. "I suspect she's an ex-babe," he opines.

"She's a *mom,* Mom," says my offspring.

Emma is tall, slim, commanding, drinks her Scotch like a man, and lives in a huge, beautiful barn of a house in the Scottish woods. She wears big jewelry, dotes on her dogs, is impatient with fools, likes to tell stories about Salvador Dali, and once spent a day in Greenwich Village searching for Motley Crüe records for her fifteen-year-old daughter.

"How about Rose?" I ask.

Rose is my landlady for the month. She is tall and cherubic and smiling but can make you shiver to your soul if she uses her schoolmarm voice. She has extensive gardens, runs two guest houses, helps run her husband's business, supervises two sons, and organizes everyone in the village, even me. I am mad about her.

"I keep telling you," says Mike, "to be a babe you have to be in your early twenties."

"Or younger," says my issue.

"And have unstudied hair and not too much makeup," I say. "And a tight butt, not-too-big-breasts, and a startled-fawn face," I say. "That cancels out most of womanhood. I have just become enormously depressed."

"Hey, listen," says Mike consolingly, "a babe is in the eye of the beholder."

A gorgeous fifteen-year-old babe walks into the pub and spots my two guys. Tousled hair, startled-fawn eyes. This is a bold babe. She makes little chitchat, starts rubbing against Mike, running her fingers through his hair, puts her hands in my boy's pockets.

"Let's go out into the moonlight," she whispers to them.

"Help!" says Mike.

"Help!" says my child.

HOW TO
GET A MAN
(I'M SERIOUS)

know what men want.

Men want a lady in the living room and a whore in the bedroom.

Men want women's hair to be fragrant and shiny and long. Long hair is feminine.

Men want women to be feminine.

The way to a man's heart is through his stomach.

Men want a gourmet cook. Men want a woman who can serve a four-course meal at a moment's notice.

Men want a woman with a sense of humor.

Men want to be mothered.

Men want smooth, firm buttocks.

Men don't like a hard, competitive, tough woman. She makes men feel threatened. If they feel threatened in one regard, they feel threatened in all regards. This way lies impotence.

Men don't want a doormat. If they can walk all over you, they won't respect you. If you want a man to marry you, be a demanding bitch.

Men want a certain air of mystery. Don't tell him where you're going, what you're doing. Smile enigmatically. Keep secrets. Have flowers with suggestive notes attached delivered to yourself and blush with confusion when he notices them.

Men want a nice set of knockers.

Men want an athletic woman, an outdoorsy woman, a woman who is in fine, muscular shape. A woman with a decent tennis serve.

Men want women who will share their interests and hobbies.

Men want a good pair of legs.

Men want well-groomed women with clean, shapely fingernails and a dainty scent.

Men want women to wear high heels so that their ass projects outward.

A man wants a woman who will understand him. A woman who knows why he gets melancholy on Sunday afternoons.

A man wants a woman with a small, trim waist.

A man wants a helpmeet.

A man wants a slut. He wants a woman who will be a tiger in bed, a woman who has a huge sexual appetite and massive erotic skill. A man wants a tireless, inventive sex-slave.

A man can't stand even a hint of desperation.

A man will want you much more when he thinks he can't have you. The way to get a man is to come on strong and then run away.

A man wants a woman he can show off to his friends.

A man wants a woman who can hold her liquor.

"Oh, blow me," says this man who was in my bed a minute ago and is now reading over my shoulder.

"Nice talk," I say, "very nice."

"How dare you decide what *men* want? As if all men were the same. Don't you realize how demeaning that is?"

"I know, don't you think I know? I'm just trying to whip the reader into a frenzy of rebellion! I'm bludgeoning her with the conventional wisdom! I don't mean a word of it, okay?"

"Blow me anyway," he says, climbing back into bed.

The thing is, when women get lonely and scared we *believe things*.

Say it's raining outside, you're coming home from your boring office-temp job, you throw open the door to your apartment and collapse into a frenzy of tears.

You just can't bear the idea of spending one more hideous evening on your sofa, staring at your same old knickknacks, misting your goddamned philodendron, popping another stupid Lean Cuisine in the microwave, and sniffling over another episode of *Murphy Brown*. You need a life. You need a man. Or you'll grow crazy.

You call your Aunt Susan. She tells you to buy a garter belt and seamed stockings and wear red lipstick.

You read a magazine which tells you to match your body language to his, and to use positive imaging. You practice picturing every aspect of the man of your dreams so that he will ring your doorbell, preferably within ten seconds.

You read a self-help book which gives you a fifteen-step program at the end of which you're supposed to realize that wanting a man is just an addiction and a stupid addiction at that.

Your head swims with man-getting information. Your brain is so jangled with advice and instructions that you get dizzy and have to put your head between your legs.

What to do?

Okay, pay attention now: I have the ultimate man-getting advice. You don't have to listen to anybody else. Just listen to me. Okay, here's what you do:

Nothing.

If he's the wrong man, you can turn yourself inside out with wiles and perfume and French-maid's outfits and nothing will work. You'll never get him, you'll never keep him, you don't have a chance.

If he's the right man, you can have greasy hair, spinach in your teeth, and your skirt on inside out, and he'll still be entranced and follow you to the ends of the earth.

You don't have to believe me, but what I say is absolutely true. You just have to follow your own personal, weird, goofy little star and some poor sucker is going to come along and die for you.

Let me tell you about Nora, who was heartbroken. She hadn't had a real boyfriend in about ten years, and the man she had been dating and crazy about had just vanished. She was depressed, discouraged, devastated. She couldn't understand why men never noticed her.

"Maybe it's the way you dress," I said.

"What's wrong with the way I dress?" she asked.

"Well, like right now you look like you're wearing a series of lampshades. Is there a body under there?"

"This is the way we dressed in Kansas."

"We're not in Kansas anymore, Toto. Buy a miniskirt. Show some cleavage. Men like that."

Stubborn girl wouldn't listen. Soon she didn't have to.

Mr. Perfect reappeared. "I miss you," he told her. "I miss those ratbag outfits of yours." That was a year ago. They are now discussing marriage.

Everybody's different. Some men (okay, only a few) hate garter belts. Some hate all makeup and adore enormous, clunky shoes. Some men wouldn't even look at Michelle Pfeiffer if she appeared at their door in a negligee and begged for it. Men, yes even men, are human. And you can't second-guess a human being. Try and make a science of romance one minute, the next minute you're checking into a loony bin.

That man over there in my bed? I used to doll myself up. One Tuesday morning I went to the post office in ratty sweats, zero makeup, and my hair a frazzle. There he was.

"Don't look at me!" I shrieked, hiding behind the wanted posters.

He looked at me. "You looked really adorable," he said, and kissed me. His eyes shone so I knew he meant it.

Okay, the second part of my advice is just as simple but infinitely harder:

To get a man, you have to be ready for a man.

Taking a man into your life is an enormous risk. Can you open your heart to a man, can you be trusting and vulnerable knowing that you're also opening yourself up to the possibility of rejection and heartbreak? Can you withstand rejection and heartbreak? Can you let another person inside your defenses, let him know who you really are and what you're really like, knowing that he might someday leave you? Can you bear it?

No, neither can I. But I'm trying. It's quite a trick to build up your defenses against heartbreak and yet not be defensive against men. And the trick is to develop self-confidence. Which is quite a trick, especially when you're feeling needy and desperate.

But be brave. Have a good look at yourself. Are you torturing yourself for your singleness? Punishing yourself for your alleged failure? Eating hundreds of thousands of M&Ms to atone for your neediness and desperation?

Our society has made a practice of punishing its victims. Not only are women being punished (still!) for the feminist movement, but, even worse, they are being flayed alive for feeling weak and dependent and in need of love. Society has taught women to hate themselves.

Society sucks. Pay it no mind. Of course you feel lonely and desperate and want love! You're human! Wanting love is an honorable wish!

When you stop practicing self-hatred, when you start feeling affection for yourself and your little ways, when you are able to follow that weird and goofy little star of yours, then your fears and defenses fall from you like thistledown. Then you're ready for a man.

And then the nightmare begins.

SHE WANTS
MONEY?

There are two types of women in the world, and I am not acquainted with one type at all.

"Do you want to date a man with money?" I asked.

"What the hell for?" Rita asked back. "He'd just want to boss me around."

"Would that mean he'd be wearing a suit and tie?" wondered Cleo. "Because I couldn't take that."

"I want to make my own money," said a very pregnant Nessa. "I couldn't ask my husband to compromise his work."

"You mean someone who would pay his share of the meal?" asked Lynn.

"You mean someone who would pay his share of the rent?" asked Erin.

Personally, I have never even *known,* let alone slept with, a rich man. Neither have any of my friends, although one married a guy when he was poor, and now the guy is rich.

Yet, in response to my "I Wish I Were a Man" column, I got a bevy of letters from men, telling me it was no picnic to be them at all; all the girls wanted guys with Porsches and hefty investment portfolios. One guy even wrote, "Come on, did you ever date a guy with less money than you? I think not."

I think so. I have never dated a guy who had *more* money than I. (But enough about my dating.) After a vast amount of thought and searching for cash-obsessed bimbos, I have formulated that two-types-of-women theory: There are Professional Girls, and then there are Amateur Girls. We're talking about two entirely different species.

Professional Girls are desperate for a boyfriend with a platinum Amex card. Amateur Girls are desperate for a boyfriend who can deliver a good punchline.

Professional Girls consider beauty salons as necessary as breathing. Amateur Girls have been known to take the kitchen shears to their hair in PMS-induced frenzy.

Professional Girls pay someone to slather hot wax on their crotch and rip off half their pubic hair in order to have a perfect "bikini line." Amateur Girls cry and tremble and diet at the thought of anyone seeing them in a bathing suit.

Professional Girls want security. Amateur Girls want hot sex.

Other Amateur Girls and I have been saddened by the knowledge that most men want Professional Girls.

Oh yes, you do. I have been to cocktail lounges all over the land. I have been to parties. I have worked in offices. And I have beat my breast in anguished frenzy while watching men ooze around that woman with the perfectly streaked blond hair and the pearlized eye shadow. You always go bonkers for this Professional Girl, oh yes, you do.

And meanwhile we Amateurs stand there, discreetly trying to pull our pantyhose back up, vague mascara smudges under our eyes, deciding then and there to read that awful self-help book which we think tells us "be a bitch and men will love you."

Oh God, don't get me started.

This difference between the species is not simply grooming. Nor is it a psychological phenomenon. Sure, Professional Girls are ballbusters, but not because their fathers spoiled them rotten or their mothers were icy. The difference is political.

Professional Girls exist solely in the mainstream of society. They've bought the whole cloth of traditional mores. In the deepest recesses of their souls, they firmly believe that men have been placed on this earth to take care of them. And they fully expect and want to be taken care of. Most of their actions are directly related to the goal of having someone else pay the bills.

Whereas the Amateurs have taken that critical step back and looked at the whole deal. And it frightens us. We don't want to be taken care of, because we have noticed that when someone else pays the rent, we lose autonomy, we are no longer the captains of our souls. Somebody may expect us to have dinner on the table at 6:00 P.M. sharp, and maybe we've decided to take French lessons that evening. Sure, we want to throw our lot in with a man, but we've got this niggling notion of being an equal partner. We don't want to feel trapped.

Although we may truly want to be beautiful and desirable, it is not quite our overriding obsession, we don't need beauty to snare a meal ticket. So we'll forget to get our hair cut and feel too lazy to go to the gym, and the next thing we know the men are clustered around that goddammed blond. We're not perfect sex objects because we don't regard men as success objects.

So if you guys are finding your love lives ridiculous because of a temporary or permanent lack of funds, maybe you're looking in the wrong direction. Maybe you'll have to change your politics.

Consider a different way of life, a life in which your woman often has a run in her stocking. A life where you might have to learn how to make a white sauce and diaper a baby. A life where the bed isn't always made, where your shirts lie unironed for weeks, where you can't find a single clean sock.

Come on, it might not be so bad. If you suddenly decide to quit being a $400,000-a-year mergers-and-acquisitions lawyer and write that novel you've always felt you had in you, nobody will come at you with a meat cleaver. Somebody may instead pull up her socks and start a successful greeting card business so that you can still spend Easter in St. Croix and the kids can have shoes.

Yes, you may have to abdicate being king-of-all-you-survey (often a tract house on a quarter acre) and feel like you're living in some kind of hippie-commie-commune, for Christ's sake, but won't it be nice to know that your woman is with you because she loves you and your cute neck, not because if she leaves you she'll lose her powder-blue Capri and her French Provincial bedroom suite?

Next time you're on the prowl, avoid the streaky-haired blond with the pearlized eye shadow. Look behind a pillar for the girl with the string of toilet paper stuck to her heel.

REJECTION:
THE NEW FRONTIER

've stopped thinking men are martians now that I've nursed several of them through getting it up to ask a girl for a date. They go insane.

First a fellow has to decide whether it's worth it. Why go through torture to ask out a girl who will never be the love of one's life, the mother of one's children, the sex kitten of one's universe? A man still wants to kill himself if a dippy sap of a girl says fuck off.

Then, after he does enormous reconnaissance work and finally decides she might be worth it, this man has to make a gigantic pretzel of a mental contortion and convince himself he *doesn't care* if the potential love of his life says, "Go out with you? *You?* Are you mental?" Otherwise he'd never have the courage to make that hideous phone call:

"Hi Norma, it's Stephen."

"Hi Stephen. How are you?"

"We met at the museum, remember? At the Michel-angelo . . ."

"Yes. I know which Stephen this is."

"You sure?"

It's pathetic. I once talked Ned, whom I love like family, through three months of courage-gathering. The minute he went for this girl, he discovered he is the ugliest geek in the world (he is totally handsome) and too tedious to live (he is brilliant). Every day I had to hear about what she said, didn't say, the perfume from her dress. About how he just couldn't bring himself to . . .

"Ned," I said finally, on a Friday. "If you haven't asked her out by next Wednesday at 6:00 P.M., *I'm* calling her. I am not bluffing. I will do it."

He did it. They are now engaged.

Thus I have finally proved my theory. There's only one reason men have been so resistant to the feminist movement, one reason they haven't greeted with open arms the idea that women are their equals: It's too fucking painful to ask an equal out on a date. The rejection becomes unbearable.

If you think women are lower on the food chain, maybe on par with the moose, it's a lot easier to find out her plans for next Friday night. That's why men were such carefree casanovas until 1969, the year women stopped being chicks. Who cared if a chick said no? What did she know?

I'm happy to see that, like women, your new man can't deal with rejection at all. I mean, even a little. He won't even talk about it. It's the last taboo topic.

Like at dinner with my guys only last night. These are guys who will talk about and compare penis sizes at the table. Guys who will with equanimity discuss whether they like a finger up their ass or not. Guys who will recount childhood traumas as amusing anecdotes. Guys who will cheerfully say "nipple" to anyone.

"Guys," I said, "what are your feelings about rejection?"

They went all weird, changed the subject. I brought the subject back. They flatly refused to speak. Oh, one of them talked about a moonlit moment in Tanzania or somewhere, but it was just a one-night-stand who didn't want a second night.

"No, no," I said. "What about when you've been seeing someone for a while, a month, a year, and then she doesn't want you anymore? Come on, tell."

The guys stared at their coffee spoons and turned blue. They wanted me dead. I gave up. But I was fascinated. What is it about rejection that makes it so hard to talk about?

There are two types of rejection. The first is a blow to the ego, the second a blow to one's actual *self.*

Ego rejection we get about as regularly as lunch. A client hates our presentation. A loan officer wonders who we think we're kidding. A casting director says, "That was fabulous! Next?" A girl with a great profile says, "No, I'm sorry, I'm busy for the next three months."

This kind of rejection is as damaging as your level of self-esteem. If you're a conceited snot, you just shrug and decide the client's a moron, the loan officer's a mutant, the casting director's corrupt. (You'll also decide that the girl with the great profile is clearly a lesbian, but you'll feel it more, since everyone's sexual ego is their most tender vulnerability.) But if you have low self-esteem, any and all ego rejection will simply confirm your fears and you'll go on your moody, suicidal way.

Rejection of self is the killer, major surgery of the soul. You've let your barriers down. Your thoughts and feelings and visions and revisions are no longer bottled lonely and weird within yourself, but are now flowing freely and happily through that psychic window that opens between you and your beloved.

This communion with another is better than a shot of heroin, better than a month in Maui, better than winning the lottery. It's what we (secretly) live for, yearn for. We want to talk in shorthand with someone, want to be able to glance across the room at a party and know someone gets the joke.

When that someone who gets the joke doesn't want to play anymore, we're devastated. We feel 70 percent dead. This is the kind of rejection that no one wants to talk about. Or think about.

Because not only is this rejection horrendously painful, it's humiliating. We're not supposed to care. We're supposed to be groovy and independent, it's the law.

There is a reason that Albert Brooks's line in *Broadcast News* was the most famous and oft-quoted line in 1987–88. "Wouldn't it be great if desperation were attractive?" Albert said. "If needy were a turn-on?"

Everybody with a brain fell over and died for this line because Albert in his brave and whiny way voiced everybody's shameful little secret. We're all needy, we're all desperate, we're all terrified of revealing our sickening dependency. We'll do anything not to appear ridiculous.

Not to stand there like a fool while the loved one, turning toward the window, says, "That is not what I meant at all. That is not it, at all."

It is time to pull rejection, kicking and screaming, from the closet. We must be able to discuss it, point and laugh at it. We must be brave and take risks with our hearts and not care when the eternal footman snickers. We must dare to eat a peach.

What do we have to lose besides everything?

FAIRY-TALE POISON

We're at a poetry reading, me and Duane, and this wispy, ethereal girl comes up to us. "Can I sit here?" she asks. "Sure," we say, and move over. So she sits and kind of spreads herself out in a way that makes my intuition prickle. I watch her and wait.

"How much does beer cost?" she asks us. We don't know, exactly. She rummages in her bag and pulls out a bottle and crouches. "I brought my own. Hide me, okay? Don't let them see me." Duane, I notice, is becoming awash with protective feeling. I'm not.

Did we know where a phone was? Did we know of any apartments she could rent? Could we save her seat? So we save her seat three times, or at least Duane does, I'm ready to grab an Uzi.

"Let's go now, okay?" I say.

"We can't go," he says. "We've got to watch that girl's purse until she comes back."

"Did she *ask* us to watch her purse?"

"Well, she left it there." He stares fretfully at the large tapestry bag, its contents half-spilling on the floor.

"I hate that girl," I say.

"Why are you being such a bitch?"

"How dare she sashay in here and expect us to take care of her?"

"Oh come on, is it gonna hurt us to be nice?"

"Yes, fuck you, it is," I say.

"Clarissa, why are you lying on the dining room table?"

"Sshh, Mommy, I'm Snow White and I'm sleeping for years and years."

"Why, Clarissa?"

"So that Prince Charming can ride up on his white horse and wake me with a kiss. I have to keep very still, Mommy."

"Clarissa, dear, I don't think Prince Charming's going to ride his horse into our dining room."

"He might, you never know."

"How about if I wake you with a kiss?"

"Don't be silly, Mommy, you're not a man. You can't rescue me."

"Okay honey, but try not to scratch the varnish."

Sometimes when I go to the deli there's a woman, often middle-aged, in front of me giving the deli guy holy hell. First she has to taste the corned beef. She doesn't like it and makes him open a fresh one, but that one's too fatty, she asked for lean, didn't she? And what about coffee filters? She knows they're in the back of the store, but she forgot them, okay? So could he get them for her now? Okay, yes, that's it, no, maybe she needs some aspirin. And maybe some cornflakes. And didn't she say half a pound of Swiss? The deli guy looks bewildered as he does her bidding while the customers behind her tap their feet and mutter. He asks himself what is wrong with this woman? What does she expect from him?

We Jews would call her a *kvetch*. To me, she seems deeply, profoundly disappointed, soured, like she never got what she wanted.

Every weekday after five and before six P.M. certain car owners on the block move our cars from one side of the street to the other. Then we wait near our cars until it is legal to leave them. So I'm standing there with a couple of women, I think lesbians, talking weather and dogs. A guy pulls into the last vacant space. A woman in a straw hat with a ribbon dangling down the back runs up to him.

"That's my space! Honestly, I was just about to pull my car in there! I always have that space! You have to let me!"

"Now that is unmitigated fucking gall," I say.

"Ten to one he goes for it," Freda says.

"Come on, nobody's that much of a yutz," says Joan.

The guy shrugs and grins sheepishly, puts his car into gear, and pulls out. Straw hat grins and rushes triumphantly to her car.

"She'll never get it in there, her car's twice the size of his!" I say.

"She'll beg prettily and get everyone else to move their cars, you just watch," says Freda.

And that's exactly what she does.

"Wow," says Joan, "if they had manipulation olympics, she'd definitely place."

* * *

"But why can't I do it myself, Mommy?"

"Because dear, it's not ladylike. If he does it again, you call your father, or your brother. They can take care of that bully."

"But Mom, it was *my* bike. It should be me who punches him in the nose."

"Baby, would Cinderella punch a boy in the nose?"

"I just can't cope!" Sara was crying.

"Look, Sara," said Jill. "You left Mark because you said you wanted to be independent. I don't mind you sleeping on my couch for five months. But you have to pay your own goddammed phone bill."

"But I had that big dermatologist's bill. And then I ruined my only decent pair of shoes and had to buy another pair . . ."

"Look, Sara, I just can't keep picking up your slack. Why should I? I've got enough problems."

"But don't you see? I just can't . . ."

"I know, cope. Maybe you'd better go back to Mark."

"Well, I still think you're mean," said Duane.

"You don't understand!" I whined. "Women like that give women a bad name! And you guys, you're so stupid, you go for that kind of babe in a big way, that poor, soft, take-care-of-me type, and then when she takes *you* for everything you're worth you're shocked, you're horrified, you blame our entire sex."

"You're just jealous," said Duane.

MEN WHO LOVE
TOO LITTLE

"Just tell her I have no feelings. Just tell her I'm a prick and she doesn't need a guy like me in her life," Hank said.

"I suppose I'd better, you ratbag. You flirt with her, you know," I said.

"I can't help it. She's a great girl. That's why I want her to know *immediately* what a bastard I am."

The boy has no shame. He's my pal. It has come to my attention that I have a lot of pals who are without women in their lives. I wanted to know why, I asked them, the results are disquieting.

Hank is abnormally handsome, blond, and tall. At the artists-and-writers softball game in Easthampton last summer every girl in the stands said to every other girl, "Who's the hunk in center field?" Went to Harvard, wrote a book, was all we found out. Later, when we became inseparable, I found out he had once been the perfect, monogamous boyfriend for seven years until his girlfriend dumped him. Now he only dates models, to whom he's cold.

"I have no feelings," says Hank. "As Yeats said, 'Too much sacrifice can make a stone of the heart.' The only amendment I would make to that is 'If you're lucky.' Too many people continue to be victimized by the world of feeling. That world is genuinely silly to me. I listen to the lyrics of those songs, which in times of heartache I thought were filled with the essential meaning of life—they are now utterly ludicrous to me. They're goofier than the Flintstones."

"You're very sick," I said, and he giggled happily.

"At least I know I've fallen from grace," he said. "But from the deepest regions of that cavity that we used to call my soul, I honestly don't feel negative. I would expect more of the reaction that body builders get from their audiences—oohs and aaahhs."

My buddy Sam, whom I'm with more than anybody, is deeply funny, a cartoonist with a cheerfully evil glint in his eye. He's as steady as a rock, he rarely leaves his house, he hasn't had a girlfriend in maybe ten years. One of my friends went all silly when she met him, and he liked her too, but he avoided her madly from then on. Why, Sam?

"It's just so much easier not to bother. Life is just complicated enough already without having to deal with someone else who's wanting to be intimate. It's easier to escape into escapism. To build up a lot of obsessions about trivial things that you can have illusions of control over. Baseball stats, crazy rotisserie leagues, poker, bird-watching . . ."

"So you're a control freak. I never realized."

"It's not so much control I want but avoidance of noncontrol. I don't want someone controlling me. I'm just making this up as I go along. You just do what feels best and you figure it out later."

Readers, I have to admit that when I decided to write this I thought I could be all-knowing and smug about fear of intimacy and the callowness of men. But right now, at this paragraph, I'm beginning to wonder about women. I hope I feel more confident soon.

There's Victor, my English mate. Sweetest guy, will do anything for anyone. Most of my friends, including me, have had crushes on Victor. I don't think he noticed. He dates, looks for Ms. Right, she's never there.

"I'm very bad at presenting myself as a romantic possibility," says Victor. "I'm expected to act as a male predator. This 'smolder into my eyes, please' attitude is a denial of intelligence. I simply can't do it, it's insulting.

"I was one of those people who suddenly had to get sensitive in the '70s, and was enormously relieved. I never was a beer-chugging bloke; I thrived in that period. I've watched it all change, I've watched it all get a haircut. People are acting like they're back in the '50s. We're afraid we fucked up with all that self-exploration we did. You can't take away knowledge, and it's dangerous to pretend you never had it.

"We're not innocent, we've lost confidence in our feelings. At least I have. If I'm attracted to somebody I act like a complete fool."

Maybe I just know unhappy people but I couldn't believe how eager all these guys were to talk about it, to explain themselves, to justify their positions. And their depth of despair is beyond anything I've heard from the girls.

Listen to Brian, who has lately become famous as a writer-socialite in New York, who is enormously sexy, whose wife left him for another man, whose next lover tortured him viciously, and who hasn't had a relationship since the '70s:

"During and at the breakup of a relationship you experience the only true pain you suffer in life. It's not like hunger and poverty, those are physical and you can deal with them. But that turmoil, anxiety, jealousy, and crushing pain only come from a relationship. It's emotional and physical."

"But what about loneliness?"

"In order to be alone you have to like yourself, be content. I have hundreds of people I see constantly. I have physical companionship every night. I'm never lonely. I don't make a commitment, I don't break a commitment, which of course, people always do."

What's happening here? These guys have given up!

My theory is that not all traumas happen in childhood. A profound hurt can change your life irreparably. And if this kind of damage just lies there festering in your psyche, you'll never get better.

You have to grieve, go through the same period of mourning that you'd do if a loved one died, let those grisly feelings happen. Then start over again.

But why start over again? Is it simply a biological trick to keep the race alive, this romance business?

Hank says, "Not having romantic feelings is like having all the good aspects of a retirement home. You feel yourself above a rather demeaning and ultimately pointless fray."

"But what about closeness, and family, and being connected?"

"You're speaking a foreign language," he said.

I know women confused the hell out of men in the past few decades. Men got angry, hurt. Men have a history of not showing their feelings.

Maybe we were too harsh.

Dear Problem Lady:

I just found out last week that my boyfriend of five years has been having an affair for the past two. I broke up with him immediately. I am not in a very good mood.

Don't worry, this isn't going to be a letter of rationalization, about how he's not so bad really and just kind of neurotic and fucked up and had a lousy childhood and anyway it's probably my own fault for not being understanding enough, for not being a good enough girlfriend, for not giving him enough blowjobs. I've thought all these things and more in the panic of the last three days. If I could only convince myself it was my fault instead of his, then I could stay with him and my world wouldn't have to be shattered.

When I wasn't justifying his behavior so I wouldn't have to leave him, I was justifying his behavior so I wouldn't have to kill him. Yesterday I was actually rushing out of my apartment with a hammer—I wanted to see how his nose would look smashed across the front of his face. It took two burly roommates to restrain me.

Okay, I haven't murdered him and I haven't gone back with him—the two biggest risks of painful breakup—but I have decided I hate half my friends. Okay, maybe not half, but at least three.

They knew about it! They knew he was sleeping with, and then rolling over and fondling the nipples of, another woman! They knew he took this other woman to Hawaii! Hawaii! He took me to Atlantic City once. Where I lost $150, and let me tell you, the mood I'm in I'm even blaming him for that, the scumbag.

And my friends just sat back and merrily let him be this way!

They found out, you see, because one of them saw him with her and he confessed the whole business. Then they discussed it and decided discretion was the better part of friendship. They all say the same thing: "We didn't think it was our place. We didn't want to hurt you. We hoped he'd get over it soon."

I think that's just crap. I think if a true friend sees her friend being put in a situation that's going to humiliate her, that's going to make her suicidal and homicidal, he or she should warn that friend as soon as possible. Two years! He was fucking someone else for two fucking years!

Someone, I might add, whose name is Tiffany.

P.G.

Dear P.G.:

Exactly when were they supposed to tell you? Right away? After two weeks? A month?

There is a problem here. Sometimes, although definitely not in this case, the person is not a total rat-bastard. Human beings are not monogamous. Not even swans are monogamous. (There was a piece in the Times *recently about how these scurrilous fowls, always thought to be faithful and true, are just incredibly sneaky. In fact, the* Times *went on, there doesn't seem to be any species that is monogamous, except possibly paramecium.)*

At first, it probably wasn't clear to your friends whether your boyfriend was just a nice guy having a violent attack of rat-bastardhood, or if he indeed is a complete rat-bastard. And why tell until they were sure?

I think they should have told you after three months. Three months is the cut-off date. After three months of infidelity, a person must break it off with one of the parties or he (or she) should be convicted of intense narcissistic cruelty and sent to prison.

But give your friends the benefit of the doubt. They probably dithered, trying to decide what the hell to do, nervous about telling you, afraid you'd hate them for being bearers of bad news, afraid the whole thing would backfire and you'd take him back and cut them off instead. This has been known to happen.

Also, I'm sorry to say, they probably enjoyed it in a sick, soap-opera sort of way. Just a little. They can't help themselves, they're human, and humans love a vicarious drama.

Don't transfer your hate for your boyfriend to your friends. Just tell them not to be so stupid next time. Not that there will be a next time. Certainly not.

PROBLEM LADY

Dear Problem Lady:

So I'm a fashion designer and I just won a big award and my daughter forgot to set the alarm clock so when the phone rings this morning someone says, "Hello, Virginia, you're on the air," and I was suddenly on the radio in Cleveland. Meanwhile at that very moment the doorbell rings and it's these two huge men come to install some carpet and I buzz them in in midquestion and there they are in my bedroom while I'm in my nightgown on the radio with Cleveland and they move all the furniture out of my bedroom and I hang up the phone finally and see that my bedroom is bare and all the furniture is blocking the hallway to the rest of the apartment and the two huge men say, "We've got a problem, we can't install your carpet because your door is too low. You have to get a carpenter over here right now. It's not our problem, miss, and we're going to leave right now." And I become hysterical because they're yelling at me and I'm in my nightgown and they need to saw an inch off the bottom of my door and I can't get to the kitchen and they're leaving and then the phone rings and it's my ex-boyfriend whom I said I never want to see again because he's a nightmare.

And he has a saw, and he comes right over, and he deals with the two huge men. Suddenly everything's fine.

Is this a sign? Should I take him back?

VIRGINIA

Dear Virginia:

That is the most original rationalization I ever heard in my life.

PROBLEM LADY

WOMEN
AND
MEN

LOVE-JUNKIES:
FACT OR
BEST-SELLER?

You should know what we've been reading lately, so when we go all weird in an entirely new way you don't have cardiac arrest.

There is a big best-seller unappetizingly entitled *Women Who Love Too Much*. Everywhere I go, women are just finishing, just starting, or getting the courage to buy this mighty tome. "You should read it," everyone said to me. "It will change your life."

"Absolutely never," I said, since I hate all self-help books. I feel that self-help books are a contradiction in form. All books should only be read for pleasure; books are read so that you can jump into another person's mind and live in their thoughts. Having some pimple-brain without any sense of humor or the absurd tell me how to live my life is not my idea of reading. It is an ultimately unhealthy act.

But I bought *Women Who Love Too Much,* to understand the frenzy. I took to my bed with it, and by page fifteen I was violently crunching sunflower seeds all over the sheets while compulsively turning the pages and nodding my head in recognition. I empathized with Jill, my heart bled for Trudi, I became hopelessly entangled with Lisa, and identified to the point of mania with Melanie. I discovered that I am a victim of a disease: I am addicted to love.

The book's basic premise is that many women relive the pain and horror of their unhappy childhoods by recreating the patterns forged by their mothers and fathers—they become addicted to abusive, destructive behavior because it is the only behavior they know, the only behavior that feels comfortable to them. Robin Norwood, the author, an earnest, evangelical soul, believes that love-addiction can only be cured in the same way alcoholism can be cured—by following programs based along the lines of Alcoholics Anonymous.

Therapy won't work, Norwood cautioned, and I felt horrible. If you don't follow the ten steps to recovery you're simply practicing denial, she went on. I wanted to die.

I went on in this vein for weeks, hostile yet obsessed, doing things like pedaling madly on a stationary bike in the gym next to Rita, who is now a member of AA, and whining.

"She says we have to go to support groups once a week at least," I said, "that we'll never be able to handle this problem on our own, even with the help of a therapist. Where are the Love Anonymous meetings being held? I've never even heard of one."

"Start one of your own," said Rita.

"When? At two in the morning, when I'm finally finished with my work for the day? I have therapy, I have the gym, I have Alexander technique classes, I have my son's orthodonture problems, not to mention running an entire household and career on my own. Who has the time?"

"Your own recovery has to be your first priority," said Rita smoothly.

I just don't want to sit around in a roomful of people who only know each other by their first names and say, "He called me again this morning, he says he wants to marry me, but *I* know it's because *he* knows I'm not available." This would be so undignified!

Just when I was beginning to settle down, I was told by everybody to read the series of articles in the *Atlantic Monthly,* and I was again knocked for a loop. It seems that all my problems in love relations would be solved if only I could stop projecting hidden parts of my personality on my partners.

"I don't know," I said to my pal Cleo, who was really excited about these new perceptions. "I just don't identify. I know I'm supposed to, I know I'm probably just blocking, but I don't feel I fit the patterns."

"Oh, I do," she said confidently. "I'm definitely the female hysteric attached to the withdrawn man. No question about it. If I can get my boyfriend to read the piece . . ."

She did, and they had an enormous fight about exactly who was projecting what onto whom. I was impressed by the sophistication of that battle. I have never yet been able to get a man to admit he even *has* an unconscious.

I would like to write a book about women who work at it too much. My image of the sexes at the moment is that women are reading, thinking, agonizing, looking for patterns, delving deep into the far recesses of the unconscious, while men are whistling vague little tunes and fiddling with carburetors. What I really want is a man who is so psychologically enlightened that he can take what these books and articles say are my massive neuroses in his stride and still say, "Come here, woman."

This probably won't happen, at least it hasn't yet. But now at least, after reading, I know what kind of man I must look for: a guy who doesn't excite me with passion, who doesn't make my blood run thick with lust and longing. A guy who will be my pal, who approves of me and supports me and who is not afraid of his feelings.

I know this is right, because I feel the same aversion that I feel about eating beansprouts. I want Mallomars, I want troublesome men.

And I'm not particularly proud of myself, but here's what I think. I think the hell with it. I'm tired of trying and looking and turning myself inside out. There's too damned much of this soul-searching going on, and I find it subjugating. I may well be love-addicted, since my childhood was absolutely crazy and miserable, but I *know* I'm a victim of the times, and the times are very harsh on women who a decade or so ago opted for freedom and equality over the security of relationships. The times now say that we have more chance of being shot by terrorists than marrying, that women blew it, and I say the times are fucked, and I'll live alone if I have to.

I'm reading *Anna Karenina* now, and feel much better, thank you. Tolstoy said, "Each unhappy family is unhappy in its own way," which means I don't have to fit a pattern. Anna herself says, "If it is true that there are as many minds as there are heads, then there are as many kinds of love as there are hearts."

Who am I to believe? Robin Norwood or Tolstoy?

ANATOMY OF
A DATE

"He thought maybe we should have lunch instead," I said.

"You're right, you're fucked, it's over," Brendan said.

"I know," I said. "I can't believe it. I feel awful."

"Come on! Even Darryl Strawberry only hits one out of three! Listen, you got a lot of wood on the ball, you hit a long line drive, it was caught at the wall."

"I got to first base. I got to fucking second base."

"Then you were thrown out on a fielder's choice. Do me a favor. Run this lunch thing by other people. Let me know if any asshole is fool enough to tell you it's not over. But don't kid yourself. It's fucking over."

Okay, here's how it started: Somebody told me that Mr.   139

Date thought I had a cute ass. Then somebody told him I had a crush on him. I did not have a crush on him, and have since discovered he never told anyone I had a cute ass, he said I had a *Joycean* ass. As in James Joyce, as in some specific ass found in *Ulysses*. Which doesn't mean cute, which isn't necessarily a compliment. Thus when we met again at a black-tie affair, he in a tux and me in a gown, and we danced and almost kissed, we were already thick with misinformation.

Afterwards I went in my gown to a coffee shop with our mutual friend James.

"He has a great apartment," said James. "You could live there. I think he wants children."

"Stop! I don't know the guy! He may never even call!"

He called the next morning and we made a date.

Then he called my friend Nora and asked her what I wanted in a relationship, and was I a good or evil person?

"What?! No, come on, you're kidding. Good or evil? What does that mean?"

"That's what he asked," said Nora. "Don't ask me, I don't get anything. Men are opaque little creatures."

"Well that's great," said James when I called him. "It means he's taking this all very seriously. He takes things seriously. I guess that's why he made the date for ten days from now. Wait a minute, my downstairs neighbor is here. Hey, Laura, didn't you have an affair with ———?"

The downstairs neighbor picked up the phone. "Yes, I did. He's a nice guy. A little intense."

"Don't tell me any more," I said. "Jesus, this is going to be some weird fucking date."

So we went out on this date. So then I called everybody and told them this: He brings two bunches of half-dead daisies. Before the steak remains have been whisked away at the restau-

rant he's asking me what I want in a relationship. I blush
prettily.

"You have a lot of self-confidence to be asking this on a
first date."

"I just want to know."

So I tell him I'm a serial monogamist and want a regular
boyfriend and all that and then he says—I'm not sure about this
because the shock waves are rippling through my stomach—
that that's what he wants too, but between the time of the
fabulous party and our date he's met another girl at a wedding
and now he's all confused. I threaten to walk out. He says he
thought I would want to know and anyway this girl lives far
away and has a boyfriend and he's confused. He pays the bill
and we go out into the most cinematic street in Manhattan and
have a brawl, I'm yelling, he's yelling, it's a movie. I'm proud
of myself for not just sitting there meekly and saying, Oh, no
problem, fine, whatever. But Jesus, here I am being put into
competition with another woman before I even know this guy,
and why couldn't he keep his own council? He's screaming he
thought women wanted honesty.

"Well, there's honesty and then there's honesty," said my
shrink. "This is hurtful honesty for no reason. Don't sleep with
this guy yet."

So then we go to my apartment and by this time we're
kissing and it's great and then we spend three hours on my
couch, making out and giggling and having the best time.

"Oh *now* you tell me that," said my shrink, chuckling.

"But no sex?" asked James. "Jesus, I can't believe it. He
must have had a monster case of blue balls."

"Oh God, no sex?" asked Nora. "What ever happened to
good, old-fashioned passion?"

"This is exactly what the fuck I want to know," I said. "At

this point I am ready to throw caution to the winds I'm so turned on. But he decides he should go. WHAT DO MEN WANT? The guy walked out of here with a hard-on as big as the Ritz. It's a reversal of everything I've ever been taught! Now *they're* the fragile flowers who need true love before they take their clothes off!"

"Well, I'm glad he told you about the other girl, anyway," said James.

"You knew?!"

"Sure, he told me. I told him he better not play games with you."

"I knew too," said Nora, "Sally told me."

"I kind of like knowing, since it's the sort of thing girls do hours of detective work to find out. At least I know exactly what's going on. But then again, I don't. Because why would a guy tell you this on a first date?"

"The guy must be one crazy fuck," said Brendan.

And so it kept going. The phone lines radiated with news every day: Nora saw him at a bus stop and gave him some kind of lecture about me and James saw him at a party where he waved his hands a lot and wondered what to do about me and I heard all about all of it and my friends and I talked and talked and talked. I even called him.

"Listen, I understand Nora gave you a lecture about me."

"Oh, don't worry about that," he said. "But I wonder if instead of going to the movies on Thursday we could have lunch on Friday instead?"

And then my friends and I talked and talked some more, trying to find the reality in the clues, trying to make sense out of the senselessness that is dating today, where the spectres of death and eternal commitment hang heavy over us, where everything is fraught with too much meaning and fragility, frivolity, are lost. And the more we all talked, the more we got caught up in our own wishes and passions and dreams and the more we lost sight of the issue, the more we distorted reality.

So what do you think? Should I have just walked out of the restaurant?

SNOW
JOB

From now on I think we must have new social behavior.
From now on we have to know whether we're going on
a real date or not.

I can't take it anymore. I can't take getting any more
phone calls from any more men saying, "How about if we go
on a date Saturday night?" and what they really mean is, "How
about if we go to a party uptown and meet a lot of our friends
and then all go out for something to eat and then I go home
with someone else?" or

"How about if I take you to this odd little neighborhood
place and tell you all about my divorce and how I have no sex
drive anymore and how I don't think I'll ever be involved with
anyone ever again and then ask you for advice on how to pick
up the barmaid?" or

"How about if we go to a nightclub where I pump you for information about jobs, and then I come right out and ask you to help me get a job, then I put a lampshade on my head, then in the taxi home I get out real quick and you pick up the fare?"

I mean it's humiliating as hell to get a call for a date and not even know whether to be nervous or not. To not even be able to take that initial step and ask yourself whether you like this guy, whether you're attracted to this guy, whether you ever want to see this guy without his clothes on, because he may not even mean it.

He may want to be "just friends."

But he doesn't tell me that. No. People are modern now. So I have to do this hideous mental contortion of keeping my mind totally blank, expecting nothing, hoping for nothing, but meanwhile I have to clean my house, wash my hair, shave my legs, rub in body oil, splash on perfume, find stockings, try on ten outfits, jump on the scale a few times, blow-dry my hair, wet it and blow-dry it over again, reapply deodorant, brush my teeth for fifteen minutes, then put my hair in a ponytail. Just in case.

All the while I try keeping my mind a blank, all the while my mind refuses to be blank and keens, "Is this a date? Or not?"

I don't want to spend another ounce of my time on detective work. I don't want to analyze. I am not Sherlock Holmes, so why should I have to sift for clues?

"He's called me four times this week, does that mean something?"

"When I see him, he's always touching me—his hand on my arm, his arm around my shoulder. He leans so close to me our foreheads touch. He kisses me goodbye right on the lips. Does this mean something?"

"My friends tell me he's always talking about how adorable

I am, he brings me up in conversation all the time, so what does that mean?"

And so I try on ten outfits, trying inanely to look good, to look sexy, but at the same time I want to look regular, like nothing at all is going on. And then I feel so pathetic.

Because I might be being played for a fool. Because I let myself be thrown off-balance. When a man (or, I would guess, a woman) is acting in a seductive manner, it's hard to retain equilibrium.

There was recently a very dull man who just kept at me. Calling. Flattering. Calling again. Bringing flowers!

"He's boring, Mom, he puts me to sleep," said my kid.

"I know, kid," I said, "I'm not interested."

But eventually I succumbed. I thought that if anyone was doing this much pursuing, I should stop being so judgmental, I should open my heart. After all, the ones I chose for myself were often passionate but completely insane. Maybe what I considered tedious was just normal. So I talked myself into it.

We went to a party uptown where we met some friends and my date invited them all to eat with us. After which he kissed me goodnight and got in a cab with a tall brunette and a small blond and the small blond told me the next day that he and the brunette got out of the cab together and went into her building.

When I asked him about this, he looked blank and said he thought we were "just friends." Jeez.

I wanted to blame my own neuroses. It's much easier if it's your fault, then you can just go to the shrink, get better, and life will be wonderful. So I wanted to think I misread the clues, or in some way acted in a repellent manner so he had no choice but to hate me.

But it happens too much to too many people. It happens to really nice people without even one self-destructive synapse in their brains. They think they're dating when they're only being taken for a stroll.

We are so modern and sophisticated that we no longer have prescribed courting behavior. No longer do our parents get to say, "And what are your intentions, young man?" No longer do we know that if a person calls on Tuesday to ask us out for Saturday, his interest is romantic. Without the old rules, it is a free-for-all, it is so easy to be misled.

Without these old rules the door has been opened to a whole new arena for hostility and abuse between the sexes. I think a man or a woman who leads you to believe that he/she is passionately interested when he/she isn't is passive-aggressive in a particularly noxious way.

Passive-aggressive means that you figure out a way to do really nasty things and then if anybody calls you on it you can say, "Who, me? Why I was only . . . " Passive-aggressive means that your behavior causes other people to make the moves toward their own destruction, while you just sit back, smoke a joint, and watch. Passive-aggression is sneaky, wimpy hatred. In the old days, women like this were called "prick-teasers." I refuse to think up a name for the modern male equivalent.

But some seductive people, I am sure, are innocent. Maybe they come from the South, where to flirt madly is the same as breathing. Maybe they're simply hapless and self-absorbed. Maybe they're insecure and want to try real hard to make everyone in the world love them.

Which is why we must come up with new rules. Signals. So we know what to do. It's much too scary to ask, "Dinner? Does that mean you want to sleep with me?" because who could just calmly answer, "Yes, of course," or, even worse, "Um, well, no." We need rules to save face.

Meanwhile, my new rule is to never believe a person is interested until you feel his tongue down your throat.

FANTASY
KILLS

I t was love at first sight. The man who walked into the Lone
Star Cafe was handsome—nicely built, prematurely gray, tall,
clean-shaven, blue-eyed. He smiled at me. A big, "Hi there,
cutie" smile. Then he stood right next to me at the bar. Rita,
three stools down, gave me a meaningful look. Cleo, two tables
over, nodded approval. Irma Thomas, primo New Orleans
chanteuse, was belting "You Can Have My Husband But Please
Don't Fuck with My Man."

And here's what, I swear, immediately went through my
head: "He looks too clean-cut for this place. Too . . . nice.
That's okay. That's really good. I want nice. He looks open.
Maybe too open. Just a touch of the sensitive vegetarian. But
definitely intelligent, definitely. Oooh, nice eyelashes. Biceps
very pleasant. Butt . . . well, not the greatest, too sedentary,
but I could live with it. Another smile! This is serious; this guy

is a mover! Do I look good tonight? Did I put on mascara? I'll twist around just a little, show him I'm interested . . . Where would we live? This guy, I can tell, likes plants. Big leafy plants. Trees, in fact. A big loft downtown? The country? Will I have to move to the country? I'll probably have to make him wheat-germ shakes for breakfast. Will he want a banana in it? Does he want children soon? It will have to be soon."

Through the crowd a sinuous long-haired girl snaked. She went up to my future husband, turned her back to him, grabbed both his forearms, pulled his body snug next to hers. He leaned against her and watched the music and would never be mine. I looked at Cleo, she was outraged. Rita shrugged, rueful and philosophical.

But I had to laugh. In the space of thirty seconds, standing next to a total stranger, I had, in my head, fallen in love, forgiven flaws, made a commitment, moved to the country, tried to become vegetarian, and had two children. Could this constitute the world's record in insane fantasizing?

Okay, tell me this: Say Snake Girl had never appeared. Say the guy had talked to me. Said something like, "God, I just love that song!" Then what? I would have been so seized up with my fantasy, so sure that my romantic future lay in the balance of my first few words, that I probably would have said either, "We'll get all her albums, darling," or, "Say, what's your sign?" The guy then would have looked at me fishily, shrugged, and run away.

Romantic fantasy kills. It's dangerous. Don't take it lightly, it can ruin your life. It will cause you to say foolish and inappropriate things to semi- or even total strangers. It will make you pay intense attention to the most casual of flirtations. It will lead you to invest your emotions in the shakiest of futures.

Consciousness destroys the act. Or, as Yogi Berra put it,

"You can't think and hit at the same time." You meet a girl. She has nice legs, she's pretty, she gets your jokes. If you're the kind of joker who then decides, "That's it, she'll be my future wife if only I can win her," you're bound to lose. Because you'll have a hell of a time being natural and spontaneous with this girl, with internal expectations clogging your brain. Everything will take on enormous proportions. You'll be living spun-sugar dreams of bliss in your head, which will cause you to make insanely portentous remarks every time you speak and to stumble over your feet every time you try to take her in your arms. The girl will get away.

Or maybe she won't get away. Maybe she'll stick around and turn into a real person. This will make you crazy. She will become so prosaic! She'll get hungry and petulant when she gets her period, need root canal, and have a morbid fear of tents. You had meanwhile been dreaming of an ethereal yet rugged girl and will be filled with disgust at her perfidy in misleading you, at the fantasy not coming vaguely close to the reality, and you will dump her. That's where fantasizing gets you.

Here is Heimel's Law: Anything you fantasize about won't come true. So just cut it out.

Why (oh, why) do we do it? I think that fantasies are stillborn feelings. We all have a need to love another person. But some of us can't do it. Maybe we've had our hearts broken too much or too recently. Maybe we're generally fearful. Maybe we're all twisted up inside and think nobody who really knew us would have us on a bet. Which leaves all those love feelings with nowhere to go. They swirl around inside us, building up steam. We tell ourselves fairy tales about some wonderful prince or princess who will make our dreams come true and we pretend this can really happen. Then, when we meet somebody even vaguely attractive, we make a fatal leap.

All those pent-up feelings immediately attach themselves to this person.

But they're only fantasies, and they blind us. I know a man who falls in love four times a week and hasn't had a girlfriend in seven years. I know a woman who can obsess for months about someone she's never even spoken to, she hasn't had a boyfriend in ten years. Fantasies are self-destructive.

Trust me, I know. I have, off and on, been a fantasy maniac all my life. Every time I've had my heart broken, the next two years are riddled with dreams of knights in shining leather.

To identify fantasies, I do the phone-call test. Here's how it goes: Say the guy I'm interested in doesn't call me when he says he's going to. (All of you do that, not calling when you're supposed to is a trait definitely attached to the Y chromosome.) If I go mental, stay home and stare at the phone until my eyes cross, bite all my fingernails off and end up lying on the bed curled in a little miserable ball, I'm in the throes of a fantasy.

But if, the next time he calls I can manage to say, "Yo! You didn't call me last Tuesday, you ratbag!" then I am a well woman. Then I am healthy and clear-eyed and free to fall in love.

Here's my cure for fantasy-mania: Go out with everyone, especially people who are unsuitable. Last week I went out with a twenty-one-year-old college student (my son is appalled, but fuck him), a graduate student, an actor, and an unemployed Irishman. None of them have a hope in hell of being Mr. Right, so I can be natural with them. When they don't call on schedule, I'm only mildly piqued. But meanwhile, since I really like these guys, all my churning love-feelings are finding limited, temporary outlets, and when a potential Mr. Right comes along I won't leap all over him and gibber.

This could make all the difference.

THE TERRORS OF
CASUAL SEX

Big crisis! Cleo had sex! And it was unbelievably great! Now she wanted to jump out a window!

But instead she just sat there in the West Beach Cafe, her face buried in her hands, shaking her head and muttering repeatedly, "What have I done?"

"Well," I said, "what *have* you done?"

"You made me call this guy I hardly know . . . "

"Me? I simply said here you were in L.A. staying in a luxurious bungalow at a very fancy hotel and that everybody knows that the only thing to do under such circumstances is . . . "

"Get laid. I saw the reasoning. So I call this guy I picked up at a party last year, this guy I had sex with once, dinner with once, talked on the phone with maybe four times.

In short, a guy who I hardly knew and rarely thought about . . . "

"And he came right over . . . "

"That he did. And we had *tremendous* sex. It was beyond wonderful. It may have been the best sex I've ever had in my life."

"Oh, no," said Rita, who had arrived without us noticing. "This is a catastrophe."

"Sit down," said Cleo. "I'll buy. This may be my last meal on earth."

We sat in gloomy silence for five minutes.

"Listen," I finally piped up, "it may not be so bad. We're modern women."

"Fat chance," said Rita.

"Do you notice how my eyes keep darting to the door every time it opens?" asked Cleo. "That's because I called him this afternoon, calculating when he would be out so I could just leave a message on his machine, a message I composed and recomposed in my head for an hour and a half. In fact, here it is, word for word: 'Hi, it's Cleo. I'm in town for longer than I expected, so if you're in the mood come over to the West Beach tonight after eight. Goodbye.'"

"Very nice and straightforward," I said supportively. Rita groaned.

"My heart jumps into my throat every time that goddammed door opens," said Cleo. "I'm tapping both feet spastically under the table, and just looking at the bread is making me nauseous."

We lapsed back into silence. Then Brendan arrived and took in our morosity. "What?" he asked.

"I've just made an excursion into the world of casual sex," Cleo explained.

"You got laid? Congratulations."

"A guy I hardly knew," said Cleo. "And now I think I'm madly in love with him and I might die if he doesn't come through the door this second and I want to have his children."

"Just because he had his dick in you?" Brendan wondered. "Jesus, am I glad I'm not a broad."

"Listen buddy, there's no such thing as casual sex," a beautiful movie star named Teri leaned over from the next table to say. We of course applauded.

"Everybody knows that men are not just another sex, they are another species," said Rita.

"No," I said, "men aren't even from the same planet. For men, love and sex are two separate things."

"Listen," said Cleo, "even if the sex is bad, for at least a nanosecond we believe that it's destiny and marriage and true love forever. And if the sex is great, we're total goners. Look at me. Yesterday I was simply horny. Today I am obsessed. It's some kind of biological imperative."

"Of course it is," said Rita. "It's an instinct that is buried deep in our reptilian brains. We pretend to be modern, but our biology goes back to the Stone Age. We're the ones that have the babies. We want a man to go out and hunt for food and build us fires while we gestate . . ."

"Fucking bullshit," said Brendan. "You just don't like to fuck as much as guys."

General uproar.

"Women don't have a truly adventurous and playful taste for sex," he continued, unabashed. "You want this thing with conditions. Men unconditionally want sex, without prerequisites. You need this goofy-ass love shit. And this sensation of yours gets you people into trouble. You'd be better off without it. Snap out of it, that would be my position."

A curly-haired comedian came walking along. "Just because I want a hamburger doesn't mean I have to marry the waitress," he intoned cryptically while passing.

The waitress came over. "That guy at the third table wants to buy you a drink," she told Rita. "Very cute, wearing a wedding ring."

"Tell him I'm a lesbian," said Rita.

"Listen," I said, "we want sex just as much as guys. It's just that as soon as we get turned on the fantasies start flooding in. I was at a party last night and there was this really cute Italian guy I was crazy for. I wanted to sleep with him a lot, so I made up this whole endearing personality for him. Then he started bragging about his money and ancestry. Then he made a big push to go home with me, but the thought of him touching me made me nauseous, because he was an asshole."

"Who the fuck cares?" said Brendan. "You should have taken him home and made him wear five condoms."

"Who? What?" said Herb, who had just walked in.

"We're talking about how women can't have sex unless we think we're in love," said Cleo morbidly.

"I will admit it's better when you are in love," said Brendan. "Much, much better."

"You mean to say," said Herb, "you don't have fantasies about running around and screwing everything in sight, with no guilt, no shame, no consequences, and the next day forgetting who it was and finding someone else?"

"No," we said.

"Huh," said Herb. "I guess it's because women have the babies and they have a limited supply of eggs. Men have billions of sperm that they constantly replenish. For women sex always has consequences. It's not really fair."

"You can say that again," said Cleo. And then he walked in the room and she lit up like a marquee.

THE DEADLINESS
OF DUOS

They are everywhere, they are a plague on our houses. They spring from the deep abysses of this city's rancid darkness to frighten the simple citizenry. Their eyes gleam red with eager malice as they prowl and drool through the gutters and alleys of our streets. They are a poisonous epidemic, leaving disease and decay in their wake. They are a scourge.

Couples. I hate them. They make me puke.

You think I'm bitter? Of course I'm bitter! How would you feel if every time you walked four blocks to the bookstore you encountered approximately sixteen couples holding hands and staring mistily into each other's eyes, gold wedding bands glinting in the sun? Why don't they just slap me in the face?

If you're not from Manhattan you may think I'm bonkers.

In other parts of the country couples, especially married ones, know how to treat each other: with good-natured hostility, progressing steadily toward simple hatred.

In Boise, for example, Herb will call his wife, Blanche, his ball and chain, Blanche will intentionally burn the pork chops and develop a mad crush on the meter-reader. In Tulsa, Jimmy Bob and Charlene will have to be pried apart at the Liar's Saloon, before Charlene's grip on Jimmy Bob's throat becomes terminal.

This is normal, this is the true nature of marriage. You fall in love, you become dependent upon each other, you resent this dependency, you freak out. Before you know it you're either divorced or you've tenaciously fought the dark and self-ish side of your natures and love conquers all for the time being. Marriage is an endless cycle of love and fury, passion and revulsion.

But not in Manhattan. These people are thrilled to death with themselves.

It's about AIDS, of course. And the new conservatism. And just plain, bloody-minded perversity. In Manhattan, marriage is a trend. Couples kiss over their arugula and radicchio salads. They fondle each other's genitals while devouring their pasta puttanesca. By the time the tiramisu arrives, they've slid under the table.

Oh, God, the incessant smugness that radiates like beacons from these twits! The constant "we"-speak! The hideous complacency, nay, maliciousness, with which they treat their single friends!

"We're so happy!" a close relation who just dumped her husband and married another man said recently. "Aren't we happy, bunny? You should try it, you know."

And so sanctimonious. Suddenly every member of a couple realizes that all his/her life he/she has secretly yearned for monogamy, that all those nights prowling the bars and clubs, all those passionate and furtive sexual dalliances in his/her past, well, that wasn't really him/her. He/she is really into monogamy, into intimacy, into real estate and child-rearing. It's enough to put you to sleep for a decade.

What's even worse is that I feel left out. I want to be an asshole like everyone else. I want to come home to someone besides two interminably necking teenagers and one prancing-in-circles little dog. I want to go with someone to Italy, and when I get there I want a hotel room with a king-sized bed instead of two singles. I want a joint checking account. I want to file a joint return. I want couples to stop looking at me as if I were a pitiful dweeb. It's hard to keep out of the fray of social pressure, not to feel sorry for yourself when others do.

So I feel sorry for myself. I especially feel sorry for myself when I'm with people who have, against all odds, found each other and are deeply in love and not just trendy. I know two such couples. I was sitting in a cab with one such the other night and it killed me. They kept grinning and looking tender. A hand was on a knee. They were together and I was separate and it caused such a sick, demented yearning, such an astringent feeling of loneliness that I felt a deep crash in the pit of my stomach.

I remember love and closeness, but it was always strenuous for me because I was insane and frightened and if a man went loopy over me it brought out my mean streak. I have been lousy with suspicion and distrust and had a penchant for drama and plate-throwing.

I have finally figured out the rudiments of how to love somebody, too late. There are no men my age, and if there are, they want twenty-two-year-olds to bear their children. Will I ever be able to practice this loving?

"No," says my friend Brendan. "Shut the fuck up and get used to living alone. You don't have a chance."

"I am used to living alone," I said. "I just would prefer not to in the biggest way."

"You know 95 percent of guys are assholes," said Brendan.

"Maybe, but at least 80 percent of women are assholes too."

"So that makes 5 percent nonasshole men for 20 percent nonasshole women, and all of them are insulated by the assholes all around them. Assuming you're not an asshole . . ."

"Thank you very much."

"You're totally fucked."

This is true. But at least I'm not desperate. What if I were? What if every morning when I woke there was a horrible thud of fear in my brain, what if every day were filled with anxiety and a fevered search for Mr. Right? What if every night concluded with me crying my eyes out?

I was like this once. I was taught from babyhood that men were the answer to my problems. My mother, my aunt, my grandmother worshipped men, felt a slight distaste for women. A woman was as important as the job her husband held, as the state of her kitchen counters, as the clothing on her children's backs. A woman had little or no intrinsic worth. I was never told there was an option of growing up, acquiring skill, working for a living. I was told that when I grew up I would get married and live happily ever after.

So I thank God that marriage is simply the latest trend, not a requirement. That I do not have to play the role of the gay divorcée or the woebegone spinster. That I can go into restaurants alone and not be spat upon. That nobody can arrest me if I point at these couples and laugh (hollowly).

CHEATING
SITUATIONS

et's-call-her-Margaret couldn't see out of the taxi because she was swoonily slumped against let's-call-him-Max, her head nestled into his chest as he crooned a George Jones tune into her hair.

"No, no," Margaret murmured, "this is unfair, this is cruel and unusual, this is way below the belt. Do not sing George Jones to me, I am a good girl."

"Margaret?"

"What?"

"Can we go out? Can we see each other?"

"Yes."

"You mean it?"

Margaret sat up and put her fingers into her hair so that her curls stood straight out. "Hello, I am Glenn Close," she

said.

Max, to give him credit, burst out laughing.

And thus yet another woman decided to fuck a married man.

Infidelity is such a pretty word, so light and delicate. Whereas the act itself is dark and thick with guilt, betrayal, confusion, pain, and (okay) sometimes enormous pleasure.

I know Margaret very well, but it didn't help.

"Nothing you can say will make any difference," she said. "I already know everything. I know this will end at least in tears, and possibly in agony. I know that I am being a cliché and will soon begin to hate myself and think of myself as sordid and pathetic. I know that I might soon start entertaining fruitless fantasies of him leaving his wife and us living happily ever after, and the absurdity of thinking a man who cheats on one wife will not cheat on another. I know that we are playing with a stacked deck, that he has all the aces and I have no power, that I'll never be able to pick up the phone and just call him, even if my fusebox blows up at three A.M., that he can never be there for me. I know that I am indulging in a profoundly anti-feminist act and will probably go to hell. I know I am violating the fifth commandment and that I am immoral. And I know, God help me, that I could fall in love, and that then I will really be fucked."

"But do you realize," I said, "that by filling your life and dreams with this man, you're not leaving any room for a nice, decent, single guy who will bring you flowers and propose marriage?"

"Of course," she snapped. "What am I, dumb? Don't I have a shrink? Listen, this is not a pattern of mine. I don't have a string of married men in my past." Her face was red with feeling. "I have been waiting around for that mythical single man for three years! Nobody's even kissed me in a year! And then out of nowhere this amazing guy comes, and I am struck by a lightning bolt of lust. What would *you* do?"

"Jesus, you really are fucked," I said.

These times do not well accommodate infidelity. Those loopholes that were created in the '60s and '70s have been pulled tighter than Jesse Helms' sphincter. We no longer sanction open marriages or wife-swapping. We don't pretend anymore to be not jealous. We don't casually turn the other way while our mates "find some space." The sexual revolution is over, the days of randy experimentation dead.

Because there is *that disease.* We are understandably afraid to die. But even if there weren't *that disease,* we are immersed in the neo-fifties, a time of conservatism and blind patriotism, a time of born-again Christians and TV preachers and *Fatal Attraction,* of the reglorification of the nuclear family. If *Anna Karenina* were written now, it would rocket to the top of the best-seller list.

But God or whatever it was that created the species has screwed us. We do not mate for life. Instead we have this overpowering sex drive. A crafty, irresponsible monster of a sex drive that rides roughshod over rules and morals and righteousness. A sex drive that makes fools of us all. So we can buy white wedding dresses and sharp tuxedos and order engraved matchbooks and promise in front of the entire world that we will, goddammit, be faithful for the rest of our lives, no kidding, and still some small, frightened part of our brains will be keening, "Well, anyway, I'll really try!"

No matter what our brains say, our bodies will do anything, anything, to get laid. It's bigger than all of us.

The more we try to deny the sex drive, to pretend it isn't there, the worse we will be destroyed. Witness (and laugh at) poor Jim Bakker, wretched Jimmy Swaggart. They tried like hell to put the lid on.

So who amongst us will cast the first stone at Margaret?

"I will," she says. "I will cast the first stone at myself. I am such an asshole. Why am I doing this? Women don't do this. Do they?"

"Of course we do," I said, "all the time. The most we can ever do to stop ourselves is to really, I mean really, try to be faithful, try not to go after another woman's man. To never do it lightly, or casually, or to get back at someone, or because we're bored or depressed or feeling fat. Because infidelity is serious shit. It deserves respect and fear."

"Did you hear about Beth?" she asked. "Fifteen years married to the same guy, suddenly she goes cold, can't sleep with him anymore, and she runs away with a sexy young penniless musician, and now instead of being an art patron she's waiting tables at a coffee shop?"

"Just goes to show you the lengths we will go to to get good sex," I said. "Meanwhile her husband, I happen to know, was having at least three affairs a year."

"*How* do you know?"

"Never you mind, missy. I'm just pointing out that even in this area, women are different."

PORN TO
BE WILD

ormally, Brendan is mild-mannered, the soul of consideration. But we rented some hard-core pornography, he became a monster. I stood with him in the video store, dead with embarrassment, while he went raging through the tapes and barking orders. "Hold this," he said, "and this, and this," and pretty soon I was clutching a tower of filth. He narrowed the booty down to three tapes and made me go rent them. I had to say, *Dickman and Throbbin'* out loud to another human being. Loud enough for the gay guys renting *Rear Entrance* and everyone else to hear.

"I should kill you for making me do that," I told Brendan outside. "Listen," he said, "you wanted the complete smut experience." Which is true, I did, which is why I invited five male heterosexuals over to my house to watch. I wanted to be a female fly on the wall.

What to feed them? I wondered, a fluttering hostess. Peanuts and beer, like at a football game? Genitalia shaped objects? Tacos and weiners? They didn't care. Brendan and Jerry, very excited, stuffed themselves while arguing about blowjobs. Philip, arch and detached, wouldn't eat. Mel, fidgety and quiet, had a bit of chicken. Johnny, an inscrutable Oriental, declined even drink. I popped the first tape, *Misty Beethoven,* into the VCR.

"This is going to be good, a classic," said Brendan, watching. "Fucking Paris! I rest my case."

"The lighting's terrible," said Jerry.

"Ugh, the music," said Mel.

"And the camera angles, you can't see anything!" said Jerry, who is such an aficionado he brought his VCR along to dub the movies. "Except the herpes on her lip! I can't look!"

Off came *Misty Beethoven,* on came *Three Daughters,* a femme production, made by women, which everyone liked at first, because of the music and lighting. Then they noticed that nothing was happening.

"She's got tiny, tiny tits. Tit size is real important in films," said Jerry. "Let's fast-forward."

"Once we see frontal nudity we'll slow it down," said Brendan.

"Yuck, those tits," said Jerry. "This is definitely a female film, notice she's the one who decides when the dick goes in."

"Also notice that there's not a giant dick in her asshole," said Brendan.

"They're showing pictures of makeup and china! What is this, the home shopping network?" said Jerry.

"Phil Donahue and Marlo Thomas watch this one," said Philip.

"I have better at home," said Johnny.

"I'd rather watch sports," said Mel.

They fast-forwarded. They were intent and feverish and hardly noticed me, which was fine, for I was becoming queasy.

"Vibrators for women and home porno for guys," said Brendan during the tape change. "Watersheds in beating-off history."

During *Dickman and Throbbin'* a major fight broke out. I wanted to hear the dialogue, Philip and Jerry wanted a bit of foreplay, Johnny didn't care, Mel hated the whole thing because it was shot on video, and Brendan wanted to charge through, only stopping at the straight fucking. Jerry grabbed the remote and was the victor.

"Got any cookies?" Brendan said.

"I've watched scenes from *Ebony Humpers* twenty or thirty times," said Jerry.

"Come shot!" screamed Philip.

"Yes, yes!" shouted Mel.

"Not much come," muttered Johnny.

"Probably coughed up a few wads already today. Do you think there was a fluffer involved in this production?" asked Philip.

"Got any milk?" asked Jerry.

They didn't like the mailman. "Bag defect!" intoned Brendan. "We can't look at deformed scrota," explained Jerry.

But they were amazed by John Holmes. "That's sizable," said Philip. "That looks like a prototype for a lot of dildos. Perfect veining."

"Throbbin's not exactly small either," said Johnny.

"With him, they usually have to leave three inches or so of dick outside," said Brendan. "His dick could split a girl in half. How many drugs did they have to give her to do this?"

"Maybe it's a stunt dick," said Philip.

"What? In the middle of everything they quote from the back of a ginseng bottle?" said Mel.

"Goes to show they're ignorant white people," said Johnny. "Oh, I like that. Women are very good at faking it."

I noticed that I had had my hand in front of my eyes for about ten minutes. John Holmes had frightened me. I took my hand away and noticed that the fellows were all sitting cross-legged, drinking milk and eating cookies. Brendan was actually dunking his cookie into his milk.

"There is beer available," I said. They didn't want any.

"Oh! Between the tits!" said Mel.

"Pearl necklace!" said Philip.

"The tits aren't big enough," grumbled Jerry.

"They're human tits, fuckhead," said Brendan. "They're not from the Planet Tit."

They fast-forwarded. "Hold it," shouted Jerry. "What was that? Oh never mind. I thought there was one in her ass." Back to fast-forward.

Then they got all excited about an NH blowjob. No hands. Very appealing. They then admired a girl's pointy ass. Then they decided they liked the green underpants better than the beige, which bunched. Then Brendan fell asleep, Johnny started reading a magazine, Philip and Mel started discussing football.

"No matter how good it is, have you noticed it's never good enough?" said Jerry as he packed up his machine.

I felt like a den mother, watching my friends regress to voyeur boys. It was almost sweet, their simple fascination for the purely visual, for the pointy asses and the breast size. But I'm never showing my body to anyone again. Which is okay, because after seeing these films, I never want to have sex again. Ever.

GIRLS WATCH PORN

First we all had to have a hundred cups of coffee. Then we had to admire Erin's sweater. Then we had to have a boy (my son) connect the VCR. Then we had to decide how many of us had PMS (two). Then we had to tell how many of us were estranged from our boyfriends (too many). Then we had to have a boy start the VCR. Then we started to scream.

High-pitched girl shrieking, like teenagers did for Sinatra and the Beatles, except horrified, as if teenagers saw Sinatra murdered. This seems to be what women do while watching porno movies. Eventually we settled down to mere hysteria, watching *Dickman and Throbbin'*.

"I feel like I'm eight years old and my friends like boys and I don't get it," said Cleo.

"Those are fake tits," said Rita. "She's on her back and they stick straight up. God, she doesn't have any pubic hair. And what she does have is dyed."

"I guess that's an okay blowjob," said Erin.

"How does she not vomit?" said Carla.

"He's so big," said Marta.

"And it's not even hard," said Rita, "which means it's *really* big. Oh look, she's taking responsibility for her own orgasm."

"We've all faked orgasm better than that," said Erin.

"Look how she's looking at him," said Rita.

"She's trying to get him to come any way she can," said Cleo. "She figures if she gives him a sultry glance . . ."

"A come-hither look," said Sue.

"Forget the hither, just come," said Cleo.

"She's not gonna age well," said Carla.

"Why is she doing this with her life?" asked Rita. "We're talking bladder infection with that."

"This is worse than *Nightmare on Elm Street,*" said Cleo.

"This girl has a mother and a father someplace," said Sue.

"She grew up with a father who drank and fucked her," said Erin. "She thinks this is okay."

"Oh, my God, phone sex," said Rita. "Sure, like the phone-sex girl would be dressed in a garter belt."

"Did anybody have a boyfriend who would call up and want phone sex?" said Sue.

"So tedious," said Cleo.

"I'm always wearing my granny nightgowns and knee-socks," said Rita.

"And he always asks what are you wearing," we all said.

"Is that Gael Greene's boyfriend?" wondered Marta.

Total shrieking for cunnilingus closeup. "I could never be a lesbian, that clinches it," said Cleo.

We all had our hands in front of our eyes. "But aren't we supposed to have female pride?" said Erin. "Why do we think this is gross?"

"I haven't seen a cunt so far that looks like mine," said Rita.

"I've never seen mine," said Carla.

"I have," said Erin, "but I don't think I would recognize it in a crowded room. We've been socialized not to like this. We've been trained to hate it, men have been trained to love it."

Dickman, a.k.a. John Holmes, unveiled his shaft. Screams.

"That looks like a weapon!"

"That can't be real!"

"That's attached to his body?"

"That looks like an elephant!"

"Varicose dick veins!"

"Okay now," said Rita. "You take this premise—a girl's a virgin and her mother wants these guys to give her some experience—that could be really sexy if you did it the right way, instead of this, where they're bludgeoning her to death with their penises."

"Like if it was only one guy and he was Dennis Quaid," said Cleo.

"Oh, I would like two guys," said Erin.

"Yeah, the other guy could be Sean Connery," said Rita.

"Have you noticed that there's absolutely no kissing in this movie?" said Marta.

My son came in the room. "Don't look, don't look!" we screamed. He got a magazine. "Instead of watching that, I'd buy this," he said, holding up *Sports Illustrated*'s swimsuit issue.

"That's a healthy attitude," said Cleo. "It'll make you want girls you can never have in a million years." He left.

We watched *Three Daughters,* the femme film.

"This is better, it's not as offensive," said Cleo.

"But it's not sexy," said Erin.

"Wait a minute," said Carla, "we never saw his penis!"

"It was negligible," said Marta.

"Is anybody else looking at that wallpaper?" asked Rita.

"Who ever masturbates like that?" asked Cleo.

"I never even take my clothes off," said Rita.

"And I won't even talk to myself afterwards," said Sue. "Turn this off. I don't want to see a movie more boring than my own life."

"Why don't they ever get it that boxer shorts are the most sexy?" asked Cleo.

"Blue jeans are sexy."

"When they roll up their sleeves is sexy."

"When they work on cars."

"When they concentrate on anything."

"A guitar goes a long way."

"What about shopping in a stereo store? Just kidding."

"Never when they look like they've contemplated what they're wearing."

"Someone who looks like a smart hell's angel."

"When they're a little bit dirty. Long hair."

"Blue jean jackets, whatd'ya think?"

"Yeah!"

We absolutely didn't get why they have to show semen spurting. Two of us almost gagged. A couple of us were turned on for a moment or two, but then upset by the overkill. We all hated the closeups. Three of us had severe anxiety attacks. All of us decided we like sexy books much better. So we ate lollipops and talked knitting and calmed down.

CHILDHOOD
IS POWERFUL

Pity the poor infant. Born perfect into the world from imperfect parents. At the height of his intelligence, he is completely ignorant, helpless, completely dependent on whatever maniac has charge of him at any given moment. And each of these moments is crucial, each of these moments shapes the interior landscape of the pitiful infant's psyche. He doesn't even know that he is not the whole universe. He doesn't even know he is a separate human being, he thinks his parents are simply extensions of himself. Luckily he is resilient, and learns.

You were an infant once. Your parents, being human, probably made several million mistakes with you. But you managed to pull through, to acquire language and defenses and the ability to cope with all sorts of weirdness.

And now you're probably a parent. Judging by all the commercials I see these days, everyone is this wonderful, warm, soft-focus parent, brimming with love and wisdom. Do you feel like this?

No, I didn't either. I had a colicky baby, a baby who cried all the time, a baby who made me feel helpless and scared and frustrated and resentful and okay, occasionally frighteningly angry.

But now he is a young almost-adult and people cluster around, asking me how I did it. They look at me and see an insecure mass of neuroses and miseries. Then they look at him, and see a healthy, well-adjusted, strong, kind, and compassionate kid who has already managed to have a healthier relationship in the past two years that I ever had in my whole life. And they shake their heads in wonderment and say, "How did you do it? What are your secrets?"

Listen, they're not secrets I'm proud to tell. Some of my methods happened by blind luck that turned out right. But the most important thing I've had is self-knowledge. I knew that I had royally fucked-up parents, parents who could have written a best-selling textbook called *How to Raise a Child So that She Has No Self-Esteem at All: The Parents' Guide to Twisting Your Kid's Psyche.*

If you know you're crazy, or incompetent, or merely somewhat odd, it is very important to inform your kids of this fact.

A kid, as I've said, thinks he's the center of the universe. He thinks that everything that happens is *about him.* This does not make him feel like a miniature Idi Amin, it makes him feel that everything is his fault.

You, his parent, are the most important thing in the world to him. You are his entire emotional security. If you've had a lousy day at work and are in a bad mood, he thinks he's done something terrible and you might leave him. If you've had such a lousy day that you bite off his head for spilling his milk on the floor, he is consumed with guilt and feels like the most wretched, evil creature who ever lived.

And if, heaven forbid, one of his parents leaves, he is convinced it is simply because he is an actual monster.

Therefore it is essential that you undermine your own authority and tell him the truth. "Listen kid, I know I'm being a ratbag, but I'm a fucked-up person and I've had a pisser of a day. I'm sorry" is music to a child's ear. You've let him off that desperate, scary hook.

And if a parent leaves, he *must* be informed, in so many words, that it had nothing to do with him. "Mommy still loves you, it's just that she couldn't stand the sight of me anymore," is infinitely more reassuring than, "Oh, Mommy will be back sometime soon."

By undermining your own authority, I don't mean abdicate. A kid must have discipline, he has to know there are limits. Nothing is more repulsive than an out-of-control toddler upturning all the bowls of potato chips at a cocktail party while his parents sit smiling serenely saying, "Oh, Malcolm is *so* lively today."

But limits should be logical, and carefully thought out. It is sadistic to impose discipline just for the hell of it, just to show that you're the boss. You're the boss, don't worry about that; your child's welfare must be your only criterion.

And be consistent about this or your kid will be a wreck. If you only occasionally punish him for crossing the street, he'll end up not knowing what to do, he'll end up being scared of you. He wants desperately to know what to expect. If you just happen to lash out occasionally he'll always feel off-balance, not knowing when you'll do it again. He'll cower like a mistreated dog.

Whenever possible, leave your kid alone. No, not physically alone, just let him have his way. I came upon this realization by chance, since I was a distracted, overworked single parent with very little time or inclination for policing. I never made him do his homework. I never imposed a dress-code. I told him he couldn't swear in front of his grandparents and left it at that. Now he is a self-motivated paragon. He does his homework, he is incessantly groomed, he is polite. And he doesn't take drugs. He doesn't approve of them. If you're not standing over him with a whip, he won't have to rebel.

Speaking of which, let him. I'll never forget when I was eight and I told my mother that when she ordered me to do the dishes, I felt rebellious. She beat the shit out of me. "I'll *rebellious* you!" she screamed, smashing her fist so hard on our glass table that it broke.

I think she should have made me do those fucking dishes, but I also think she should have let me hate her for it.

A kid has very strong feelings. He can feel murderous at the slamming of a door. He can become elated by the brightness of day. Give him the dignity he deserves and acknowledge his utter right to have feelings.

If you don't, he'll hate you. But the hatred of parents is unacceptable to a small child's psyche, so he'll take that anger and turn it inward against himself. Hello, I'm your child, and I'm a psycho. Let him stamp his little feet and turn blue, then make him do what you told him to.

If you have a daughter, tell her when she's about eight or nine that you're not going to marry her when she grows up. I'm serious, she might be expecting to. Be nice about it.

Whenever possible, put yourself in your kid's place. Try and feel what he feels. As much as love, empathy cures all evils.

WHAT'S IN A NAME?

Every time I tell my son how I almost named him Rio Grande, he screams horribly.

What would have become of him if he had had to walk around introducing himself as Rio? He'd either end up a Vegas croupier or heavy-metal drummer. Then when I wanted to name him Luke, my husband wouldn't let me. "They'll call him 'Luke the Puke' in school," he reasoned.

As it happens, plenty of other parents were not as perspicacious. There are hundreds of teenaged Lukes infesting New York. And a pale, pretentious bunch they are.

Yes, it's totally true, your name is your destiny. Even more than your astrological sign, more than your socioeconomic milieu, more than your dysfunctional family matrix, your name determines your entire personality.

How many poor girls, who would have been wild and raging and beautiful and free sex goddesses if only their parents had found it in their hearts to name them Isabel, instead had to stuff their poor psyches, sausagelike, into the name Heather? Heather of the baby voice, the wispy hair, the tendency toward apologetic chunkiness?

How many fine and strapping young men were turned prematurely pear-shaped windbags by the name Melvin?

Since it seems to me that this fad of child-rearing has turned into an actual trend, that babies are an increasingly popular accessory for people-on-the-go, I first want to say to stop naming your boys Max. Max is a perfectly nice name, ensuring in its owner a certain precocious sensibility, but there are enough Maxes now. Any more Maxes and the breed will go to the dogs.

Secondly, just because the vogue is now to name your child timeless, classical, boring names doesn't mean you won't produce a small and then a larger psychopath. Okay, without further ado:

WHAT TO NAME YOUR UNSUSPECTING BABY

Alice will have a will of iron and grow very beautiful. A compulsive liar.

Donna will be the sweetest and brightest of all children, then become the town drunk.

Ellen will be a projectile-vomiting infant, commit arson as a teenager, finally settle down to early-American quilt collecting.

Gloria will be an uncommonly creative child. She will grow up to advise people what colors they should wear. "You're an Autumn," she'll say, and they'll give her fifty dollars.

Jane will be straightforward, loyal, and a heroin addict.

Katherine will be the sweetest, most unselfish, most docile child imaginable. She will cost you several million dollars in therapy bills.

Lynne will spend her entire life in bed, eating sunflower seeds.

Mary will be sharp and sympathetic and has a simple wish: to destroy the universe.

Nancy will be a poignant, smoldering child. As a grownup, she will involve several baseball players in paternity suits.

Patricia will spend her entire childhood deciding between becoming a nurse or a ballerina. She'll end up a lumberjack.

Wendy, a quiet and withdrawn child, will become the first female serial killer with her own TV miniseries.

Adam will be plagued by intelligence and awkwardness and write bad checks.

Arthur will cry through his entire infancy, tear wings off flies through his childhood, then become an actor.

David will be the teacher's pet, the high school football hero and thereafter a raging alcoholic.

Don will break his mother's heart.

Fred, a kind and considerate child, will eventually have his life ruined by a go-go dancer.

John will raise weimaraners and wonder what went wrong.

Julian will feel he has no choice but to become a poet.

Kurt will just be unbelievably goofy.

Malcolm will be an insurance adjuster and make a hobby of not calling when he says he will.

Mark will be a mischievous, bright-eyed lad, then a celebrated hitman and underworld informant.

Peter will spend his formative years wanting to be a priest, then get his wish.

Robert will become abnormally attached to goats.

Sam, a melancholy child, will spend twenty years in prison.

Steve, shy and adorable, will assassinate the president.

Walter will poison the earth's water supply.

And these, I hardly need tell you, are the lucky ones.

Dear Problem Lady:

Hoo boy, am I drunk. It is like—Jeez, I am plastered!—three o'clock in the morning and life is beautiful. I mean, you should see the sky out there, black as fucking ink, murky as shit, gorgeous.

So anyway, here's what I want to know: What is love? Why does it take total possession of your heart and bone marrow and turn you inside out so that even your fucking pancreas is exposed to any moron who cares to look? Why does love frighten you and leave you wringing wet? How the hell am I supposed to cope?

I mean, is there any way not to lose yourself? Not to want to absorb every smell, every sweat droplet, every sinew of the loved one? Is there any way to hold back, to wait until it's good and constructive and healthy, to cut your losses and walk if it's turning out weird? A way not to see things through to the bitter, nerve-jangling end?

You know, maybe I'm talking about passion. Is there a difference between love and passion? If so, why? Also if so, why won't my passion attach itself to that nice flower-bringing maniac who appears whenever I want him to on my doorstep, who I could never fuck in a million years, instead of to this, this, well Jesus, you should just have a look at him yourself and you'll see what I mean.

Please help with this problem. I'm going to go throw up out the window now.

LORETTA

Dear Loretta:

Approach any random physicist, he will whip out vast numbers of equations and tell you that life and the universe are

*chaos. Humans, terrified, will fight fang and nail against this
chaos.*

*Mainly we buy things. Normal people will spend $400 on a
sheet at Porthault when the chaos fear threatens. Or run ten
miles a day. Or organize things. Or attend cocktail parties.
Collect first editions. Shoot heroin.*

*Chaos and passion are the same thing, the thread that gives
truth to our existence, which is why it is so scary. Love is slightly
different, but not always.*

*Here's all you have to do: Make sure your passion is passion,
not neurosis. Make sure it's the real thing—bloodcurdling,
mind-numbing chaos. If it is, run out and buy a great Romeo
Gigli dress as fast as you can.*

Problem Lady

Dear Problem Lady:

*I realize it's tedious of me, but I am a parent. My life is
awash with playgroups and babysitters and sprained ankles from
tripping over rubber duckies. My kid is four and he is sturdy and
jolly.*

*So everyone comes up to me and wants to know what private
school I'm sending him to. And I just turn pale and nauseous
and change the subject. And they say, "Well, it's probably too
late but if you're lucky you can get him into a marginally decent
school."*

*Fuck marginally decent schools! I don't want my kid to go
to private school. I can't stand the thought of him at Dalton or
Little Red Schoolhouse or wherever they're supposed to go. I don't
want a little snot running through my living room, telling me
all about his friends Kent and Kelly. Even if I could afford it, I
couldn't bear it.*

So my husband and I will move to the suburbs where the children don't carry knives and sell crack in the schoolyard. But tell me, will I shrivel and die without the Cottonwood Cafe, without Three Lives Books? Will I go insane if I can't go see a movie at the Quad? Am I sacrificing my own mental health for my child's?

MS. X

Dear Ms. X:

When did you move here, six months ago? Who have you been hanging around with? Martians? Rich people?

Don't you know that a prerequisite for having a decent life in New York is knowing how to play the angles? Knowing where to find a taxi at two A.M., which deli has decent potato salad, where to go to reupholster your couch, who has the best deal on a stereo, where to buy sheets, get food processors for half price and Romeo Gigli dresses for $179?

Don't you know that there are two really great public schools in Greenwich Village, where you obviously live? Have you been hiding under your sofa? Where did you get your sofa, anyway?

P.S. 3 and P.S. 41. You find the rest out for yourself.

PROBLEM LADY

THE WRITER'S
LIFE

HIGHWAY 1967 REVISITED

J ust thinking about it makes me want a joint, bad. I know,
Nancy says we should just say no, but something tells me
she spent the '60s in an Adolfo suit and an air-conditioned
room, her head under the pillow. But I was out—in the
streets with the panhandlers, sleeping in the field at Wood-
stock, marching against war, driving a VW on acid, cadging
food from folksingers, dancing in dayglo, being at be-ins—and
now every magazine has politely informed me that it's twenty
years later, and I have a powerful hankering for some grass.

Somebody once told me if you say you remember the '60s
you weren't really there. I never think about the '60s. Really.
Just like I never think about my childhood. It's simply that
everything I am right now started then.

One day I was wearing a Peter Pan collar and a circle pin

and Bob Dylan came on the radio and immediately everything I thought was my world fell into a yawning chasm and I figured something was happening here, I didn't know what it was, but then neither did my mother, and she never would, so I ran away from home.

Next thing I knew I was living with an entire rock and roll band. But I had my own room—with purple silk curtains, purple Indian spread on the bed on the floor, rush matting, and incense. I anointed my body with lemon verbena oil, wore miniskirts which barely covered my crotch, walked dreamily in torrential rains, never slept, and fell in love every day.

Girls had simple roles in the '60s: We cooked lentil casseroles and baked hash brownies. We changed the record once the guys decided whether they wanted to hear the new Cream or Procol Harum. We put mascara on draft-board-bound boys. And we kept explaining that it wasn't that we were uptight, and no, we weren't afraid of sex, we just didn't feel like it.

Listen, it wasn't anything like feminist utopia. But I remember going to a gynecologist and being fitted with an IUD. As I lay in bed, bleeding and in intense pain, I was happy as a lark. I wouldn't get pregnant! I could sleep with boys I wasn't engaged to! I didn't have to marry anybody!

Was it only the giddiness of youth, this euphoric feeling of freedom, of things breaking wide open, of nothing making the same boring sense it used to? Or was it the '60s? Were they magic like we thought they were at the time?

Yup, they were. My apartment is now overrun with sixteen-year-olds, my son and his gang. They are adorable, smart, open-hearted kids. But there is no sense of joyous possibility in their eyes, these kids are cynical bastards—Reagan sucks, society sucks, the future sucks, but they'll play the game, they have no choice.

Yet they get a gleam in their eyes when I tell them what it was like. Yes, I was in the audience when Dylan started acoustic, finished electric. Yes, Keith Moon actually spoke to me once. Yes, I saw Janis Joplin, the Beatles, the Mothers of Invention. Yes, I once sat at Jimi Hendrix's bedside. Yes, I sat in, marched, went to SDS rallies, saw Abbie Hoffman crack great jokes.

I often come home to the time-warp smell of incense, the sound of Crosby, Stills and Nash, and the sight of young bodies festooned with peace signs, tie-dye and headbands. The biggest poster in my son's room is of Jimi playing his fender strat. To them, Hendrix is *God*.

I know what these kids pine for. They want the feeling that we had back then, the feeling that there was us, and then there was *them*—the straight people. The feeling that you were either on the bus or off the bus. The feeling that good and evil were clear-cut, that those who believed that we should be in Vietnam and that guys should have short hair were evil. And, most important, the feeling that there was a good chance we would win. These days we all assume that Ollie North was lying, and know there's not a damned thing we can do about it.

Arlo Guthrie once told me, "I remember when you could look down the street and you could tell who was your friend and who wasn't. There was a six-month period there—you knew who had a roach on him. He was holdin' onto it for dear life . . . but soon after you had guys who looked exactly like you sellin' you *oregano.*"

And I remember the day we were hanging around the band's commune and Roger came in with the first press kit for a rock band (Moby Grape) any of us had ever seen. It *looked* psychedelic, yet it was done by ad people. I believe the word "hype" was coined on that very day. We felt a sinking awe, we grokked that "hippies" (a media term we adored) were about to be swallowed by the voracious maw of corporate America. The loophole we had found would soon be pulled taut, and nobody would be playing guitar for the hell of it anymore.

A couple of years ago I was with a boyfriend at one of those trendy New York nightclubs where everyone wears black leather and looks bored while they grovel shamelessly to get into the V.I.P. room.

"Why do you come here, these people are all wankers," he said.

"At least they're not *straight,*" I snapped.

"Doll," he said, "you're a moron. You still think there's such a thing as a counterculture. These people would all sell their mothers for their big break on MTV. The term 'selling out' is obsolete."

Of course he's right. I don't have to tell you about the morally bankrupt '80s, we're all living here. But I am here to incessantly testify that the '60s, contrary to popular belief, are not dead. Many of the things that we were ostracized for fighting for—civil rights, natural foods, consumer advocacy, ecological purity—are now commonplace.

And deep in the heart of every forty-year-old accountant is the secret knowledge that he was there, then. He may not admit it, he may not want to do anything about it, but he still gets a twinge of fury when he hears "Day Tripper" in Muzak, and a hidden part of his brain sings, "What a drag it is to get old" at three in the morning while he's trying to get some sleep. He knows what's been lost.

And pretty soon all those kids hanging around my apartment and their brothers and sisters all over the country may rise up with a mighty hue and cry and the '80s will be over. And we can start having fun again.

COMING OF AGE
IN CLUBLAND

I n the beginning there was CBGB, Studio 54, and the *Soho News,* and they were pretty good.

We went to CBGB and watched David Bowie listening to Patti Smith or Debbie Harry, we got stoned and drunk and went behind the stage to the thickly slimed bathrooms where the toilets overflowed onto our ankles, we didn't care. We fell in love every night and it was great.

Sometimes we went uptown to Studio 54 and sat in the second-floor lounge staring at Way Bandy's eyeliner and being wholly amazed that boys went into the girl's bathroom. You could tell when someone was fucking in one of the stalls; the whole construction would shake rhythmically. But mostly we started doing cocaine then. We found ourselves in the occasional limousine at four A.M., very naive and smug.

Approximately 20 percent of lower Manhattan spent every spare second working at the *Soho Weekly News,* staying up for thirty-six straight hours and not getting paid, throwing Exacto-blades at the publisher who deserved it, having sex and taking drugs in the basement, in the darkroom which was an aluminum shed painted to resemble a barn. We wrote our own letters to the editor, Stephen Saban decided to become a writer instead of an artist, Michael Musto wrote anonymous letters to the advice columnist, Annie Flanders held court in an inside-out sheepskin coat, headlines were decided by physical violence.

And then there was the Mudd Club, which was good, we liked it there, and upstairs at Max's, which was bad. At the Mudd Club we took part in wholesome events like Legs McNeil throwing anybody who wanted him to down the stairs and parties where giant Quaaludes hung from the ceiling. No one was fabulous exactly at the Mudd Club, we wore Betsey Johnson clothes at all times. At Max's Kansas City the Heartbreakers held siege, a group that couldn't sing and couldn't play. Johnny Thunders (guitar) and Jerry Nolan (bass) were responsible for corrupting and destroying too many girls by turning them anxious and finally into heroin addicts. Wayne County had a sex change and became Jayne. At a press party we saw Patti Smith flip out, dance across the tables kicking everyone's beer into their laps—and then she disappeared. We were staying up later and later, taking more and more drugs, we tried to keep away from Johnny and Jerry.

We went to Hurrah and listened to the bands Jim Fouratt found for us, we dressed in leather. We went backstage and watched Joey Ramone drink liquid protein. It looked like blood.

We went to Danceteria on Thirty-eighth Street, then we went to Danceteria on Twenty-first Street. We went to the

Peppermint Lounge and became extras in Susan Seidelman's *Smithereens* by accident. We skated at Roxy and had our pictures taken in compromising positions.

At the new Danceteria we noticed that we were now surrounded by clumps of intent-to-make-it-in-big-city video artists with the brains of carrots and moral integrity of fleas. Our own morality was failing exponentially with the amount of drugs in our blood.

The *Soho News,* plagued by a preponderance of assholes in high places, folded. Stephen Saban started wandering around the streets with twenty-four cents in his pocket.

Then he started working as a doorman at AM-PM, which was the downfall of everyone. Although it was luxuriously appointed upstairs, we all sat in AM-PM's basement, perched on crates of beer and indulging in impossible excesses of enormous amounts of strange chemicals and listening to John Belushi waxing lyrical on slam-dancing while draining a vial in one monster snort. We would finally stumble out into the daylight at lunchtime the next day, bemused by normal life. Celebrities started coming around in droves, which was amusing.

Then the giant purge of after-hours clubs and we were all rocked back on our heels and Stephen started working the door at Kamikaze. We didn't go in, we just hung out outside with him, watching him be evil to everyone and amassing a reputation.

Details started, Area opened, the Pyramid shocked, and we were off on another round of parties. But we were jaded, feeling a bit faint, we couldn't find our friends. We decided to stop going out for a while because it wasn't the same, we weren't the same. We stopped taking drugs.

Then the Palladium, and several clubs opening and more closing, dizzying and confusing, populated by strangers.

We're tired, spent with excess, none of this has anything

to do with downtown. Who are those debutantes in the Michael Todd Room? Which one is Cornelia Guest? Everybody we don't know wants to go to the parties, invitations to which flood our mailbox (people we never heard of are inviting us to their wedding receptions).

There is a new club opening on Fourteenth Street which features lots of overstuffed couches. That's where we'll be. We're so tired that we're almost extinct.

JUST SAY
PLEASE

I t was a lovely time. A luminous sweetness wells up in my memory, my eyes close dreamily with the feeling of lightness, of happy freedom. Compared to then, these days are storms of darkness and cruelty. I wish it were like it used to be.

Drugs. I miss them. I miss feeling good for no reason. I don't want to walk on the stairmaster until the endorphins take over and I feel I can rule the world, I want a Quaalude.

And then, if I get too sleepy, I want to snort a line to wake me up. Then, too wired, take another lude. Then maybe a hit of pot. Then can I please have a nice Valium so I can get a little rest?

I miss the time when a lovely rich lawyer fell in love with me, brought me home, and took to bringing me a breakfast tray with a rose on it and then blowing cocaine tenderly down my throat.

I miss going to a certain Chinese restaurant in L.A. where everyone did lines at the tables between courses, and if you got to know the chef, he took you in the kitchen and blew it up your nose for you.

I even miss the time when I took heroin by accident. It was the day after the blackout, the day after my birthday, a baking summer day with no electricity, and my boyfriend's decadent friend from L.A. came over and brought brown powder and we sniffed it right up. "This is really mellow coke," I murmured, sinking into my bed and staring nowhere happily. I snorted it once again on purpose, at the Mudd Club, but ended up in an alley puking hideously, as I did the accidental time.

Just as well I didn't acquire a taste for it, since my best friend at the time did, and now her face has turned to a marshmallow and she walks around in a shapeless black coat, muttering. And she was the cutest girl in New York and maybe the funniest.

I had a birthday party at the Mudd Club which I don't remember. Much. I remember Stiv Bators sitting with me, I have a picture to help. I remember John McEnroe just standing behind me and wondering if I'd invited him.

"I remember it," said Alan the other night. Six of us between the ages of thirty-six and forty-one were sitting in a car, rapt in the past, on our way to a party which signified the demise of *Details* magazine, which we knew we wouldn't enjoy. "We walked over together and you were wearing a shiny green dress, and you took a Quaalude on the way over." He started stroking my head fondly.

"I wish I had a lude right this minute," someone said.

"Even a joint would be okay," said someone else.

At the party we ran into a man who said to me, "The last

time I saw you you threw me up against the wall at the Mike Todd Room and searched every one of my pockets for cocaine." That I remember. I remember thinking he was a silly git and wanted him to feel stupid. I had some illusions then, they were grand.

I don't even like cocaine, it makes me grind my teeth and go quiet. But I miss the devilishness.

Then there was that time in L.A. with Stiv Bators at the Tropicana when I accidentally bled on his bed and he was so sweet and gentlemanly, said it didn't matter at all, don't worry, here have this lude for the plane. I walked out into the hot sun with the lude in my pocket. On the plane I took it with a double screwdriver and after the takeoff I only remember landing and feeling great. And now poor sweet Stiv has been run over and killed on foreign soil. He was from Ohio, from a town famous for rubber.

I remember interviewing a movie star, can't tell you who (Richard Gere), out of my mind on my first and last infusion of crystal meth. He thought it was hilarious.

I remember smoking DMT and being spirited up to my bedroom behind a beaded curtain by an insane Italian boy. And smoking it again at a be-in.

One day ten years ago I was walking loftily down Sixth Avenue and ran into a rock journalist (are there still such creatures?). "Last night I had some hash, then some coke, then a couple of ludes, then I think tequila, then Lester made me swig some of his cough medicine," I told him.

"Can I drink your urine?" he asked.

I remember eating a packet of morning glory seeds and waking up in the morning next to a man wearing a tuxedo and a top hat.

I remember being in love with a folksinger and staying at

the Gramercy Park Hotel when Rick Danko came in with some real live groupies. "Don't worry," I whispered to my folksinger, "I hid the drugs and the Scotch in the oven."

Oh shut up, sure I remember my boyfriend from Brandeis taking TCP and claiming he was seduced by Timothy Leary, and he is still to this day a gardener. I remember acid-crazed boys waking up in fields, babbling naked. I really remember the deaths. And I apologize for nothing and there's no excuse and I don't care. We're all clean now and many of us are dying in a far less friendly fashion. And the new hip world is bright and hard and glib and mean with bottles of Pellegrino for the table and I can't relax.

HOLIDAY
HEALING

packed my bags and left town with the kid. He always
wanted to go to the Caribbean. I didn't care much. My life
was shot.

Okay, not shot. But there comes a time in a woman's
life when too much water has gone under the bridge and
the idea of knitting seems awfully racy. When even fantasies are
too much trouble. When the prospect of being sexual seems
appalling.

My friends scoffed when I said I was never taking my
clothes off in company again. "Well, not for a year," I said. "I
may not be retired, but I'm on a leave of absence. Anybody
wants to fuck me, he can apply in June 1988."

"I'll bet you dinner at Gotham you'll get laid in the next
two months," said Rita.

"Don't be crude," I said. "We're talking about a life crisis here."

I have ironclad reasons. One is the male-shortage myth, political propaganda to make women feel desperate. Women are being pressured intensely to give up jobs and start batting their eyelashes again. Antifeminist propaganda has reached an alarming high. This depresses me. Then there are the diseases, then there is my personal life.

Maybe this has happened to you: You're demented-in-love, you spend too long finding out it will never work. Then you spend an equally long time feeling like a plant that has been bending one way toward the sun, but the light-source has changed, now it's time to start growing upright again. Please say you know what I mean. Anyway, then you feel all cold and remote if anyone even makes a peripheral pass at you, and if you decide to scratch that cold-and-remote level, you find gelatinous fear. Me in a nutshell.

Barbados is just off Trinidad, near the equator, the heat is so thick you feel as if you're being ironed. The airport is probably ten miles from our hotel, but the cab ride took about forty-five minutes, because the main highways are barely two cars wide and people walk in them, often carrying parasols or large parcels on their heads. Plenty of wild, strangely configured palms, plenty of monkeys.

We arrived at our hotel, the Colony Club, which has the best beach situation probably in the world. Overhanging trees, chaise lounges under thatched umbrellas, the bar and open-air luncheon patio right there. So you can get a thickly rummed piña colada and lie there getting gently drunk and then stroll into the Caribbean, which cradles you like a baby.

I floated and stared at the poison manichel trees and got

to feeling rickety and strange. The last thing I wanted was the tension to ooze from my body, since it was holding me together. So I got dressed and went to the police station.

"I want a driving permit, please," I said to the cutest cop I've ever seen. He took my money, stared deep into my eyes, and told me his name was Colin. Perked me right up.

The kid and I went to the flower forest and took pictures of each other. We went to the wildlife preserve where I went into shock watching a monkey carrying around her dead baby while the other monkeys tried to wrest it from her grasp. We went to Bridgetown, the capital, and looked at hideous duty-free china. We sweated like pigs and drank Banks beer, which is wonderful. I was running around as if I were in New York.

That night, while I was dressing for dinner, which you have to do in Barbados, since there don't seem to be any inelegant restaurants, the telephone rang. This was obviously a mistake, no one was allowed to call me. It was the cop.

I swear I only said I would go out with him because the tourists in Barbados are so unappealing. You don't want to talk to them; they are either plummy-voiced, affected English people or snotty Americans who condescended graciously to the natives. Horrible. So I said "Sure Colin, come right over."

He doesn't drink, he is in the habit of busting people for drugs, he lives with his mother and several siblings. "How do you like the tourists here?" I asked him.

"Is there a city in the United States called Georgia?" he wondered. "I shouldn't say this, but those people are rude. Why do they come here where the population is 90 percent black?" What could I tell him?

I don't know, it became a relationship. The sun did the inevitable and relaxed me. I bought a tiger-print sarong from a beach vendor. I snorkeled and saw the pretty fishies. Colin called three times a day, often fresh from another drug bust. We had tiffs, even. More like negotiations. About me not being where I said I'd be, about him being late.

It seemed normal, which I'm not used to. I'm used to 1987, the attitude between the sexes is basically, "I hate you and I'm going to play every game I can think of." "Oh yeah? Well, fuck you!" This vacation relationship was organic give-and-take, I started dimly remembering the way things used to be.

I was having vivid dreams and nightmares every night, to the tune of the ceiling fan. One morning I woke up, and the unhappiness which had been permeating me suddenly seemed discrete, tangible. I could almost see it—a black bundle of misery, and I was beginning to separate from it. I don't want to be like this anymore, I thought, I'm going to stop.

"I'm hungry, Mom, let's go to breakfast," said the kid. We ate papaya and pancakes and drank strong tea and decided we were too lazy to ever move again. I felt my misery floating away, off into space. Tropical strangeness.

But meanwhile I was hardly letting Colin hold my hand. Too soon it was my last night, Colin and I went walking on the beach. Every time he tried to touch me I closed up. He thought I was a maniac. I used up some courage to put my arm around his waist, where I felt a hard bulge. He wasn't glad to see me, he had a pistol in his pocket. We came to some rocks.

"Let's go skinny-dipping."

"I don't want to."

"Why not?"

What could I say? Because I'm a dried up prune? Untrusting, cynical, and frightened?

"Let's go skinny-dipping."

Reader, I looked up, at that moment a star dropped straight down from the sky. I looked at the sea, then at Colin, grinning in the dark. I started untying my sarong. What the hell, you gotta live.

FOR RENT:
EMPTY NEST

Last night I went to Nell's, the posh New York night spot, where I oozed and swarmed my way past many monolithic doormen, dozens of burly bodyguards and hundreds of the surging fashionable to get within ten feet of the stage. There I presumed upon the friendship of a poor girl who thought she would be having an entire chair to herself, sat on the two inches of hard wood she generously allotted me, waited through over an hour of having my knees smashed and my lap sat on by strangers. And why?

So I would be there at 2:30 A.M. when Prince did an "impromptu" set after his Madison Square Garden gig and then the next day I could call up my kid and say, "Guess what you missed, Mr. College Man, Mr. Off-On-Your-Own, Mr. Dormitory Resident?"

I did it, too. "I hate you," he said, and I became utterly gleeful.

Last year I kept thinking it was sort of a joke, kind of a goofy pastime, all this applying to colleges and taking S.A.T. tests and filling out forms. I didn't think it would actually *come* to anything. We'd gone through lots of major changes and crises before, but we'd always lived together, that was the constant.

It wasn't until we were actually packing the rented minivan that I went mental. "You're taking your night table! That's crazy!" I yelled, "Oh Jesus, you're taking the clock radio too? Put it back! You'll need it here!"

"Mom," he said slowly and patiently, "I'm going to be living up there. I won't be living here anymore. I need my things."

And so it finally sank in. Luckily his girlfriend was with us or I would have tried to beat the shit out of him.

After getting him settled in his new room, after touring the campus crawling with hyped-up teenagers rocking and rolling through the quad, after picking up keys and meal cards and seeing how much fun it would all be, I went to the train station to go home. I ordered a tuna melt at the snack bar. The waitress was maternal and garrulous and made my melt with care. I knew she was worried as I ate and cried all over my chips. For just that moment I really wanted to be the kind of person who could throw herself into the arms of a total stranger and say, "What should I do? How do I handle this one?"

Because I now can, I have been walking around my apartment naked. I have been taking two-hour baths. Because I no longer come home to find at least five teenaged boys sprawled throughout the living room, eating my dinner and watching MTV, I now spread out all over the entire sofa and watch PBS.

I marvel at new miracles—the exact amount of food in the refrigerator on a given night is still there the next morning. Dirty dishes no longer multiply exponentially while I sleep. There is always enough milk.

And plenty of silence. No more Led Zeppelin. No more cracked adolescent howls. One day the urge to speak was bursting. So I spoke. I said, "Oh, Jeez, I must get to the dry-cleaner." Right out loud. I looked around, all embarrassed. Nothing bad happened. "But I'm not in the fucking mood," I told the air.

Turns out all my single friends have been doing this for years. Mike even gives himself pep talks in the mirror. Herb yells obscenities at the TV. I never knew this until now.

My friends have been such a help. They take me for drinks, humor me when I beg them to stay overnight, grapple me to the floor when I start chasing insanely inappropriate men. "You have to be watched like a hawk right now," Brendan told me. "You're at your most vulnerable and therefore completely insane." Women who have been through it before tell me that I'm normal, that they too were inconsolable. "Even though I was looking forward to the last one leaving, I was a zombie for months," my mother-in-law confided.

Sundays I devote to major sobbing. Sunday used to be the day we would both wake up late, hurl cheerful insults at each other, go out and eat French toast and argue over which movie we might see. Now I just line up the hankies and let rip. It is hell. I hate it. I am pathetic.

I stare at photos, caress worn-out tee-shirts. I dust off old memories: when he was an enormously fat baby who crawled around on the floor and sucked on bananas, getting banana in his ears, between his toes, up his nose. That day he had been home from grammar school for hours, we were playing Monopoly, and he casually said, "Oh Mom, I forgot to tell you, I have head lice." The terrifying time he had blood poisoning. The time he caught the last out for the Little League championship. The time I left him alone when I shouldn't have. The time I screamed at him for no reason. The time I didn't listen when he really needed me.

The fucking guilt! When you're a young mother, your child is not the most priceless treasure in the world, your child is just your child. Each day is not precious, it's just another day. How are we to know that it all ends, that they go off on their own, a living history of all our slights, bad moods, pointed and pointless lusts, irrational distractions and just plain motherly cruelty? Now that now I know how to do it right, I want to start over.

Last night I saw on TV that they acquitted this witch who smothered her newborns because she had post-partum depression. I would have given $100 to have my kid there so I could have said "That's the fucking limit!" to him, and he would have said "Somebody should smother *her,*" and we could have communed in our outrage.

I go through entire days of fury. Never before have I separated from someone without a giant fight, and I don't know how to do it. I'm just aching to punch someone in the nose.

But not him. He's doing exactly what's he's supposed to. He's off, starting his own life, fending for himself. Last night on the phone he told me he got his own "courtesy card" from the supermarket. He has his own checking account. This is big stuff.

On the train going home, after that big bout of grief, I uncovered a new feeling. One little part of my brain was actually congratulating me. "Well, that's done," the little part said.

"You've got through the teething, the training, the babysitters, the report cards, the tantrums, the baseball cards. You've cleared the hurdles, averted the perils. It's been a mighty job, but it's finished. You've raised a fine human being." I was proud. Then I felt like shit again.

WE ATTEND
A WEDDING

M aybe it was the stress of flying halfway or so across the country, maybe it was the ambivalence that a wedding brings out in women of a certain age, but we were out for blood that Thursday night.

Sammy and Jean were getting married in Texas, a couple dozen of us had flown from New York and Los Angeles to end up that night in a small fishing cottage next to a bayou, where we played full-contact charades to unwind.

"You call 'How Could You Believe Me When I Said I Loved You When You Know I've Been a Liar All My Life' a song title?" Rhoda yelled at Cleo. "It's got twenty-one words! Sadist!"

"Oh, really?" said Cleo coldly, "and I suppose 'Spaceships from the Planet Iagra' is a popular best-seller, moron?"

The bride-to-be had to send everyone to bed.

"Here's my dress," said Rita in our motel room, which contained a ceiling fan. She pulled out a pearl-gray A-line, simple and elegant, and then an electric-blue bundle of sequins "Or this, in case I'm feeling rowdy."

"Here's mine," said Cleo. "I know it's got puffy sleeves and a million colors and looks like a little girl's party dress, but it's the only one that spoke to me."

I duly showed my pink-and-black taffeta with too much cleavage. "So tomorrow's the barbecue," I said, "and the next day's the bridesmaids' luncheon and the wedding that night, and then on Sunday we nap and have another party. That's four separate but equal outfits. Festive."

"I'm exhausted," said Rita, "personally I think that when somebody gets married they should give parties for us."

"Kind of as a consolation prize, a good idea," said Cleo. "You may still be a spinster, but here's a lovely tea service."

"We're not spinsters," I said. "Those five years I spent as a housewife are etched in my brain, and Rita's had dozens of husbands."

"Well I was only married for a few months when I was eighteen," said Cleo, "and I don't think that counts. I'm a spinster. And do you know what my chances of getting married again are? I've been reading magazines. They tell me the probability is greater that I will get swooped up by a flying saucer tonight than that I will ever marry."

"Poor baby," I clucked. "What are you wearing to the luncheon?"

"Ah, my purple, I think. All the girls are sleeping at Myrtle's, the town's beautician. A slumber party."

"Weddings turn the world into teenagers," grumbled Rita as she removed the last vestiges of eye makeup and got into bed. "Good night, hons."

"Don't think bitter thoughts, dear," I said.

We moved into Myrtle's after the barbecue. She was a fine, handsome, middle-aged woman with a grand smile. "Hon," she said to everyone, "if you can't find somethin', just look for it. There's plenty of cakes and pies in the kitchen, all the neighborhood women have been baking for you-all's coming. Drink some wine."

"She's got five-hundred-dollar patchwork quilts on all her beds," I whispered to Rhoda, who was frantically looking for her blow-dryer and simultaneously patching a run in her stockings with nail polish.

"Weddings turn me berserko," she said, "and there have been so goddammed many lately. Why is everybody suddenly getting married?"

"*People* and *Newsweek* both say none of us have a chance in hell of getting married again, now we're in our mid-thirties."

"What do they know? They're crazy! They're full of shit! All my girlfriends have lost their marbles and got themselves husbands! They've all forgot the '70s, when they fully and maturely came to terms with the fact that marriage was a male plot to keep us in our place!"

"I want to get married again," I said placidly.

"Why?" asked Rhoda and Rita and Cleo.

"Because I like the intimacy and I want another baby."

"We notice how long you kept your husband first time around," said Rita.

"You just want a bunch of blenders," said Cleo.

Jean, the bride herself, blew in like a tornado, all nerves and excitement. We gave her a Valium and a glass of wine and made her lie down on Myrtle's fluffy carpet, where we took turns massaging her from head to toe.

"I want to get married every day of my life," Jean said hazily. "I'll never get so much attention again."

"You just wait till tomorrow, honey," said Myrtle, "when

we give you a Jacuzzi bubble-bath and iron your dress and I do your hair and Sarah does your makeup and Mona does your flowers and you turn into a princess."

The next day held only one calamity: The bride's mother turned on the water for her bath, the shower came on instead, all over her new coif. Myrtle had to make an emergency housecall.

After the bridesmaids' luncheon, when thirty-one women dressed in ladylike fashion got pissed as newts on Great Western champagne and caroused mightily at eleven A.M., I found myself with Cleo and Rhoda helping Jean to make a fruit cascade in her mother's garden.

"Gimme about twenty more toothpicks," I said as I tried to make a bunch of grapes adhere to a pineapple, which was itself skewered to a watermelon, "I'm so excited I'm about to die."

"We all are," said Cleo. "Look at Sammy, our blushing groom, over there, pretending to be normal. He's in a coma."

"My blue spike heels will never make it across this lawn during the wedding march," Rhoda prophesied gloomily.

A wedding turns people tribal. The night was soft and thick and pungent with eucalyptus. All the girls were fiercely protective, gathered around Jean—our prize, our angel in white sequins. The men in their penguin suits hovered around Sammy, keeping him erect and functioning.

Jean marched to her fate across her mama's lawn. We cried. Then later we laughed and ate shrimp and got drunk and many of us made shameful advances toward strangers.

Jean threw her bouquet, Susie happily caught it. Jean threw her garter, and all the men stood there, watching it arc into the air, then ran away.

"Who are they kidding?" Rita wondered.

"Nobody," I answered.

WHAT, NO COLUMN?

Okay, I meant to write a column this week, fully intended to, and then I did. Really good column. The dog ate it. I came home, grabbed a beer, stripped off my damp dress, patted the dog and . . . there was a mangled bit of paper jutting from the corner of her mouth. I pried the paper from her fang, read the phrase "maniac defensive tackle who f" and knew all was lost.

"Tits!" I cried, "what have you done?" The dog's name is Tits. She is not my dog. My friend E. Jean, who just married, has a husband who has a lease which says no dogs. I love a dog. I even love dog breath. I took Tits. This dog was the best cattle dog in Montana. People across the state would call up and try to borrow Tits to herd the cows. So you could say a superstar ate my column. I have tried with her. She could only eat so many rawhide bones, and when she did, I would moo enticingly and prance into the bathroom, trying to elicit herding. She just looked at me reproachfully in that way they have. She wanted to ride the range, and here she was in Chelsea. Plus she's a girl dog, similar to girl humans, who when insecure are oblique. "After all," her melting glance told me, "better I eat your column than your new shoes."

So, a column. Was about to write it last night but, really, a person needs *The New York Times* at two A.M., just to keep abreast, and who should be coming out of the deli but Danny and you tell me how I could say, "So sorry, got a column to write" to a close, darling friend whose dad just died. So we walked to my stoop and smoked a million cigarettes while Tits lay belly-up, hoping for scratching. Turns out Danny is afraid to go to California, because every time he does, disasters happen. Gets there one minute, next minute gets a phone call about dad. Goes again, totals his car. Goes again, finds a terminally ill friend, who needs it? Nobody, the world is here.

So we sat and smoked in the fetid, sweet New York night, watching the Valium pushers spill their wares into the street as he told me how he was the only Jew in the history of the earth to go white-water rafting, and how every day his eighty-year-old mother arrives in Manhattan to visit him on the arm of a green-haired punk guitarist/delivery boy, don't ask. And I'm suddenly transcendental, who could work after that?

I get up in the morning, frog-march myself to the desk, and the phone rings. (Let me tell you something about writers. You know how you sometimes call them and their answering machines tell you they're on deadline, they couldn't possibly pick up the phone? Lies, totally. Every writer will pick up the phone the instant it rings, because *we have to know*. It could be anybody. We pick up phones even when we're sleeping. I personally will ignore a phone only if I'm fighting or fucking, but some writers won't, even then.)

It's Cleo, she's on the corner with her brother, and of course I had to go join them for cappuccino, they were on the corner! Come on! Cappuccino is more integral to Manhattan than the F-train, we must have it constantly. Put a cup of even lousy, even decaf, cappuccino in front of anybody, and they immediately, compulsively tell you everything.

Cleo wanted to complain about men. (Yes, I know, we're trying not to do this anymore, we're trying to be all grown up and adult and realize *men have pain too, men have been suppressed too, they need a break right about now,* but every once in a while our brains snap and we're back there in 1971 and what the hell, it's time for a rant.

"Men never have an honest, naked feeling their whole lives," Cleo said, "and the minute they think they do, the minute some slimy, vestigial amoeba-sized emotion drifts to the surface of their consciousness, they get so pleased with themselves that this nascent sensation gets drowned in a sea of self-congratulation."

"You broads," said dark-haired he-man sitting at the next table with the *Post.* "You don't know the half of it, you don't know anything."

(Here we fucking go.)

"You're right, big fellow," I said to him, delighted to find a man whose anger is overt.

"Gloria Steinem and Phil Donahue, between them they have ruined my life. Feelings, hah!" he crashed his fist on the table.

"If you give him your phone number I'll break your nose," Cleo whispered.

Now I ask you, who can write a column when fantasizing

about the perfect rage-riddled romance? Me, of course. Great column. Then I took Tits for a big walk, during which she ate dead hot dogs from the gutter, then decided to shit in front of eight construction workers, who like nothing better than a full-lunged excrement discussion.

"She's gonna miss the paper!" "Look at all that! Whatdya feed her, Chihuahuas?" "That's it, girl, bend over, clean it up!"

They so addled me that it was only later I noticed I accidentally used my column as Tits' Portosan. It's gone forever.

HOLIDAY SUICIDES:
WHY?
WHY NOT?

On Thanksgiving day, if I wanted to, I could have watched *It's a Wonderful Life* incessantly. Could have woke up, turned on the TV, there it would be. Could have watched it over and over until finally going to sleep, all tear-stained, as Jimmy Stewart said "Do ya know me, Burt?" for the eighth, or maybe eightieth, time in one single day.

But I didn't. I only watched it once, which is probably why I am still alive.

I am convinced that *It's a Wonderful Life,* with its gruesomely heartwarming scenes of family love, with its insistence on the indomitability of the human spirit, with good triumphing so satisfyingly over evil, is singlehandedly responsible for the alarming escalation of suicides during the holiday season.

215

Think about it: Jimmy Stewart decides it would be better for everyone if he were dead. Just as he's about to jump off the bridge into black, freezing water, an angel appears. An angel with an endearing personality who proceeds to show him his value as a human being and the really astounding lengths that our neighbors will go to nurture us and give us money!

Don't you think that many of these holiday casualties are merely pretending? That they poise on window ledges, pop their heads in ovens, and gobble handfuls of Seconal fully expecting Clarence to come along and stop them? Then when he doesn't, they get *really* depressed, and jump.

Actually, anything on television from now until January 2nd is bound to make us want to die.

Every single show is almost pornographic in its graphic displays of heartwarming family encounters. In fuzzy, glowingly rich colors, television families, from 8 P.M. onward, go all misty and hug each other in complete acceptance and understanding. Unconditional love riddles the airwaves.

Well sure, there are conflicts. Freddy gets mad when he has to spend a weekend with boring old Grandpa. Mindy doesn't understand why Mom is desperate for her to be the most popular girl at the Christmas Cotillion. Natalie is miserable when sister Kate cries when Natalie tells her she's pregnant again.

But then, within the hour, we discover that *boring old Grandpa is actually a great old guy with a lot of wisdom! Mom wasn't popular as a girl, and she wants her daughter to have what she missed! Kate's husband doesn't want children, but then he comes to his senses and realizes that he's just being immature!*

And everybody cries and falls into each other's arms and all conflicts are completely resolved and there are no residual ill feelings whatsoever and someone cracks a joke and then there's a Hallmark Card commercial.

We watch these shows, then we take a look around at our own lives, and we have no choice but to kill ourselves.

Because even if we're cynical, even if we're aware that we're being manipulated, we still fall for this stuff, because we so pathetically want it to be true.

In our real lives, Christmas is when we descend into the belly of the beast. Christmas is when we go home.

We go home, our brains addled with expectations of happy endings, to the very place and the very people who turned us into slavering maniacs to begin with! Nobody's going to fall into anybody's arms in an orgy of compassion! Nobody's even going to be pleasant! The entire function of family holidays is to turn everybody's lives into a living hell!

In fact, not many people know this, but for days before we actually get to Topeka or wherever the hell we're going our families are holed up in a secret war room, complete with pins and maps and dossiers. This is where they plan strategies to ensure that they turn us blithering and homicidal.

"Now Bob, when she asks for a second glass of eggnog, look pitying and mention Alcoholics Anonymous," they say.

"Freda, when she's trying to drop off to sleep, pop into her room and ask her why she's not married yet.

"Helen, be sure to mention her ankles every chance you get.

"Harry, praise her fruitcake to the skies and then wait until she's watching you and spit it into your napkin.

"Tommy, ask her how her 'career' is coming and smirk. Let me see the smirk. No, cock that eyebrow a little higher. That's better.

"Okay, which one of us should tell her how pretty she'd look if only she pushed the hair out of her face?"

Of course there are casualties! If our actual lives even remotely resembled Christmas television specials, if we weren't so addicted to these wish-fulfillment fantasies, they'd get lousy ratings and be canceled. And we'd be free. Free!

Dear Problem Lady:

I am becoming an old maid, a spinster! I am any character in a Barbara Pym novel! I am Miss Mapp! I am Jane Marple! Please help me!

Do you know what I did the other day? I went to the Westminster Dog Show. Shopping! I played with Toy Poodles! Maltese! Yorkshire Terriers! You wouldn't believe what the Maltese looked like with all their hair up in curlers, these tiny bits of fluff being meticulously blow-dried by baby-talking men in tuxedos ("Sit still, snookies, daddy's back-combing"). Each Yorkie had its hair gathered in one little putrid bow on the top of its head—something about this, I don't know what, reminded me of those crocheted toilet-roll covers you'll often find at church bazaars. And one need only look at the dadaist puffs all over the tiny poodles to become suicidal.

Now it is true that if I happened to own a dog with hair, there would be no bows, no puffs, no curlers, there would be dreadlocks and that's that. But the point is, what am I doing shopping for dogs? It was only last summer—and I remember it so vividly, so poignantly—that I was trying on a pair of skin-tight stretch capri pants covered all over with cherries at Betsey Johnson. A very sexy man who was shopping with his girlfriend turned to me while I was trying them on and said with a voice of deep authority, "Buy them, now." So I did, and cherished them until it got too cold.

And boy is it cold. I've had sex once this year. Once. Last year I had sex several times during one week in May and that was all. The year before I had sex once. Once.

Yes, you guessed it, I'm in my late thirties, that no-man's-land of ages. My opportunities for hot, steamy, raw, unbridled action are limited to married men, teenagers, and hopelessly addled, deranged, marginally psychotic lunatics.

Have I mentioned the knitting? I've got books, patterns. I've made scarves, sweaters. One sweater even has brass buttons shaped like bulldogs.

But no needlework, and no doilies. If ever I put a doily over the back of a chair or on the arm of a sofa, I will know that all is lost and will have a friend come over and shoot me.

But still I feel an inexorable tide pulling me from what I have always been into this alien creature I am becoming.

From a girl with drawersful of black diaphanous lingerie, with a history of sexual hijinks and wildness and fucking my brains out until dawn and then going off the next night with someone else because I couldn't help myself and riding off on motorcycles and diving naked into lakes and throwing lamps in a jealous frenzy and sobbing myself to sleep over each fresh betrayal and waiting hysterically by the phone and screaming in pain during bikini waxing and . . .

Wait a minute! Hold the phone! It's all come back to me in rush, a rush very like when I had a miscarriage and they gave me a massive shot of Demerol. This spinsterhood isn't so bad after all!

I get it now. I'm entering into a new, calm, placid way of life. A life of canines and curtains. A life without the agony of sexual longing and emotional tornadoes, jealous rampages and excruciating breakups.

So what if my house smells a little funny and my kitchen starts exploding with knickknacks and the visiting clergymen who come for tea find their trousers covered with dog hair when they get home? I will be at peace. Maybe a doily wouldn't be that bad after all.

Thank you, Problem Lady, you've solved everything.

MYRNA

Dear Myrna:

Put down that Dog Fancy *magazine, sit quietly, and listen to me very carefully.*

You are a post-war baby, a Baby Boomer, a pioneer. Before you came along, women had role models, they knew how their lives would turn out, what they would turn into. But you are blessed and cursed with being the brink of change, the thin edge of the wedge.

In the past, an unmarried woman approaching forty would have two choices: She would become the fussy old babe you describe or, even worse, she would desperately apply more and more eyeshadow, expose more and more cleavage, drink more and more bourbon and laugh louder and louder at cocktail parties.

But you're not like that. You created and lived through the '60s, you've groped your way through the women's movement and its backlash. You made it up as you went along and changed society forever.

It's a minefield of stereotypes out there, but you must thread your way through them with dignity and persistence. It is your sacred duty to forge new ways, turn expectations asunder, and fuck 'em if they can't take a joke.

Don't you dare roll over and play dead.

PROBLEM LADY